12 STE
SUCC
THROUGH
SERVICE

For a complete list of Management Books 2000 titles,
visit our web-site at http://www.mb2000.com

12 STEPS TO SUCCESS THROUGH SERVICE

Dr Barrie Hopson
and Mike Scally

2000

First edition published in 1989 by Lifeskills Publishing Group
Reprinted 1990
New editions published in hardcover in 1991 by Mercury Books
and in paperback in 1992 by Mercury Books

This new edition published in 2000 by Management Books 2000 Ltd
Cowcombe House,
Cowcombe Hill,
Chalford,
Gloucestershire GL6 8HP
Tel. 01285-760722 Fax: 01285-760708
e-mail: MB2000@compuserve.com

Printed and bound in Great Britain by Biddles, Guildford

British Library Cataloguing in Publication Data is available

ISBN 1-85252-340-9

To our customers who have taught us so much about service

To our colleagues and associates who have modelled what we write about

ACKNOWLEDGEMENTS

We would like to express our appreciation to Gert Jensen and Finn Strandgaard in Scandinavia, where much of the current impetus on Quality Service (or *Service Management* as they call it) originated.

Many people have given up their time to talk to us about their quality service programmes and to give us their views on the manuscripts. We would like particularly to thank:

Tony Barnwell of Abbey National Building Society
Ladislave Suchopar, John Williams and Bob Gill of Allied Dunbar
Professor Stephen Murgatroyd of Athabasca University, Canada
Mike Bruce of British Airways
Ian Drew and Jan Walsh of British Telecom
Brian Watts of Datasolve
Mandy Tempest-Wood of Digital Equipment
Clive Graham-Leigh of Grand Metropolitan Retailing
Tom Farmer of Kwik-Fit
Ian Ferguson of London Life
Ken Aston of Lloyds Bank
Tim Chapman of Midland Bank
Ben Thompson-McCausland, Neil Pickup and Derek Booth of National and
      Provincial Building Society
Paul Goodstadt of National Westminster Bank
Bob Nelson of the BBC
Martin Morris-Coole of Selfridges
John Metcalfe and Stuart Birch of Volvo Concessionaires UK
Philip Green of Coloroll
Carole Sausman of Carole Sausman and Company
Rob Walker of Rank Xerorx UK
Linda Lash of Avis Europe
Terry Lunn and Jeff Lynn of Joshua Tetley and Sons

And finally to the businesses large and small who have allowed us to quote stories, mission statements or internal research findings:

Abbey National Building Society
Allied Dunbar
Avis
Automobile Association
Baron Kay's Tailors, Hong Kong
Body Shop
Britannia Building Society
Bryan's of Headingley, Leeds
British Midland Airways
British Airways
Boccalino's Restaurant, Edmonton, Alberta, Canada
Budget Rent-a-car
Canon
Conputeraid Services
Cray Research, UK
Dansk Shell
Derby City Hospital
Digital Equipment Company
Douglas Seaton, Yeovil
Dudley Metropolitan Authority
Eddie Bauer Stores, Seattle, USA
Ford UK
Grand Metropolitan Retailing
Glencoe Club, Calgary, Canada
Hay Group
Hi-Fi Centre, Leeds
Horizon Holidays
Hudson's Bay Company, Calgary, Canada
Jaguar
Kwik-Fit
Ladbroke Hotels
Leeds Permanent Building Society
Lex Brooklands
Light of Bengal Restaurant, Oldham
Lloyds Bank
London Life
Los Charros Restaurant, Moraira, Spain
Massingberd, Harrogate
National Westminster Bank
Penta Hotel, Heathrow

Rank Xerox
Sainsburys
Salvo's Pizza Plc
Scandinavian Airlines
Selfridges
Shebab Restaurant, Harrogate
Sheraton St Louis Hotel, USA
Solihull Metropolitan Authority
Stanley, Leeds
Tetley and Son Ltd
Toyota
Volvo Concessionaires
Westin Hotel, Calgary, Canada
4th Street Rose Restaurant, Calgary, Canada

CONTENTS

INTRODUCTION –
BACK TO BASICS!

Obsession with the customer is the single most vital factor in business success. The main priority in any business must be to win and keep the customer. Failure to do so simply means no profits, no growth, no jobs, no business! Success will come in our competitive world to those who recognise that:

- the customer is the business's biggest asset;
- the customer pays all salaries, wages and dividends;
- the customer will go where s/he receives the best attention;
- you must be your customer's best choice!

That simple idea has underpinned all great businesses in the past, and its secrets are now being sought in all corners of commerce and industry.

By Service We Progress
Burnley Building Society, 1850

It has become the great driving force in all ambitious companies. 'Putting the customer first', 'making the customer boss', is now seen as the route to gaining the competitive edge.

A new age!

We are living in the Age of Service. For millennia most people in the western world worked the land. For the last two hundred years we have earned our livings largely in manufacturing, making goods to sell. Now, the majority of workers are involved in service businesses, no longer making goods but rather doing things that other people will pay to have done. Continually, as we shop, travel, seek entertainment, use banks, buy insurance, move house, take holidays, eat out, visit garages, take legal advice, have goods repaired, employ builders or decorators, use libraries, health services and so on, we are experiencing Customer Service. We are all experts on it; we all know the difference between good and bad service when we see and feel it. Businesses, including those involved in manufacturing, now have to pay very close attention to an increasingly aware and selective group of people who have the power to make or break them. As such, the thoughts and feelings of the customer need regularly to top the boardroom agendas of any business seriously committed to success.

Feelings – a bottom-line matter!

People's feelings have not traditionally been of concern to a hard-nosed business world. The realisation now is that they are very much a bottom-line issue. Here's why.

Let us consider first the source of customer feelings. Every contact we make when we spend our money as a customer leaves us with an impression. Most of the time we hardly notice that impression, it is neutral. What has happened at the point of contact is unremarkable, neither awful nor special, and it made no impact. Sometimes however, as a customer, the way we are treated falls below our expectations. If we are ignored, treated rudely, somehow cheated or dealt with unfairly, then we emerge with negative feelings of anger, frustration or disappointment. We will not be keen to do business again with anybody who has made us feel like that! On other occasions, however, the attention we receive as a customer seems somehow special. The person dealing with us is warm, friendly and attentive; s/he treats us courteously, takes some trouble on our behalf, and appears knowledgeable about the product. After such a contact we emerge feeling good about that experience, we are pleased, appreciative and no doubt ready for more of the same. The difference between good and bad service can be very simply represented (see Diagram 1).

Good service can therefore be defined as

**Giving customers a little
more than they expect**

When that happens the outcome is that the customer leaves with positive feelings. That is of huge significance to any business because feeling good will bring a customer back and business success largely depends upon repeat business and references from existing customers to potential new customers.

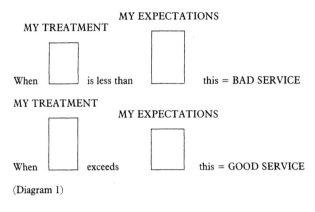

(Diagram 1)

The profits of loyalty

Businesses are becoming increasingly aware of the value of customer loyalty. If a car owner stays loyal to a particular make of car over a driving lifetime, purchasing say ten new cars in that time then s/he can be worth anything between £40,000 to £100,000 in income to the manufacturer and maybe half that to the dealer. If that satisfied customer is influential in convincing only one other friend or colleague about the car's worth, and thereby brings in another customer, then the customer's value is of course doubled. Every contact between that customer and the business should therefore be seen in that perspective. One disgruntled customer is a luxury no business can afford. This is true whatever level of business you are in. A family who spends some £30 each week at a supermarket and lives in the neighbourhood for 5 years will be worth close to £8,000 in that time. If they are treated well and speak well of the supermarket to others they can be worth many times that. Staying loyal to a bank, an insurance company, a pub or restaurant, a travel agent, or indeed any business, adds significant benefits to its bottom-line. So how a customer feels about, and talks about, a business translates into money and profit. Successful businesses need to be able to manage the customers' feelings.

Service – the idea whose time has come!

The service era has not arrived by accident, it is part of the evolutionary process of western society. Human beings have needs which

We don't know what good service is – until we don't get it!

are great drivers or motivators. Our basic needs are for food and shelter and if we lack those, we will strive resolutely to acquire them. If our basic needs are met then more sophisticated ones emerge. We then strive for more secure environments and more stability in our circumstances. Given this sense of physical well-being we are still unlikely to be content. Our needs then are for acceptance and recognition, which, if we receive them, promote our sense of worth, our positive self-esteem, which underpins and energises so many facets of our life. We want to be liked and appreciated and respond positively to signs that we are.

In the last fifty years, not only individuals but societies have worked through this hierarchy of needs. From recession and economic deprivation in the '30s, through the very destructive war and years of reconstruction which followed, our priorities were the basics, food, shelter and security. Now we are beyond the basics. With rebuilt economies most people take for granted a relatively high standard of living. Houses, cars, TVs, all manner of domestic appliances, and holidays abroad are now unremarkable. Our needs have moved beyond merely 'having', we are now in pursuit of something more sophisticated. We want very much to be treated as though we matter, we want to be valued, recognised and respected. We are hungry for the quality treatment which is a central theme of the service era. All businesses now have to be able to provide for sophisticated, discerning individuals who want more than the products they buy.

Only a little bit more

Can businesses give more and survive? *Giving people a little more than they expect* is a simple idea which involves great subtlety. If the customer is now more discerning and sophisticated, then those who serve them have to be those things also. The immediate need is to be able to 'read' your customers, to look at your business and their points of contact with it, through *their* eyes.

We all carry round expectations about the way things should be. We have ideas about the way we, or other people, ought to be treated, about standards of hygiene, about common courtesies, about fair play and value for money, about how long things decently ought to take and about many other things. We are not usually conscious of those expectations until they are either not met or exceeded.

The secret of business is to *just exceed* what your customer expects. The old pursuit used to be customer satisfaction, it should now be 'that little bit more' which results in customer pleasure or delight!

The term 'a little bit more' is an interesting one. Considering the following case:

A couple dine out in the Shebab, an Indian restaurant in Harrogate. They are made very welcome and the food is excellent and served very stylishly. They pay the bill, are helped on with their coats, and as they are leaving the woman is presented with a beautiful single red carnation in memory of their visit.

Most customers' reactions to such a final touch are very positive. It is seen as an elegant gesture which rounds off what had already been a most enjoyable evening. It is interesting to reflect, however, what would have been the reaction if, rather than one red carnation, the customer had been handed a bouquet of two dozen. What would be your reaction to that?

Most people say they would feel uneasy about that kind of gesture. They would feel suspicious because the gift seems *too* generous or over the top. Some people say that it would make you look again at the bill or believe you have been charged too much in the first place. In other words, giving people *a lot more* than they expect is likely to put them off or make them wary. It also increases your costs appreciably which can make your service so expensive that it jeopardises your business.

Good service is cost effective. The secret is to be excellent in many things that don't cost money as well as some that do!

And remember, this year's little bit more becomes next year's norm. Good service educates the customer and establishes new standards, which raises the challenge of continuous improvement.

Turning a business inside out

The idea of service management as a basis for achieving the competitive edge and building business success became the theme of the '80s. A major impetus was initiated by Jan Carlzon of Scandinavian Airlines (SAS). In the early '80s he became chief executive of the ailing airline which was losing millions per annum. His business was in trouble in times which were becoming tougher for everybody. His genius was to realise that success required an entirely different view of the business SAS was in. He observed that SAS staff were preoccupied with aircraft, airport terminals, timetables, computers, baggage equipment, catering arrangements etc. All the thinking went:

> **From inside the company
> out to the customer**

This was also the pattern in all the airlines with which SAS competed. They too designed from the inside out.

Carlzon's genius was simply to get everybody in the airline to base everything they did on another formula:

> **Ask: what do our
> customers want?**
>
> **Then manage, plan, organise, train
> and work to give the customers what
> they want and a little bit more**

SAS redesigned from the outside in! With that revolutionary formula Carlzon turned round SAS performance from a £5m loss to a £75m profit in three years. The philosophy of business success based on a dedication to service was born (some would say reborn!). The competitive edge was increasingly difficult to achieve simply in terms of having a better product. It was now to be achieved by 'managing the customers' experience'. If you gave them a real quality experience then you became:

The customers' best choice!

Any business which *did* that was likely to become very successful.

Turning the pyramid upside down!

Part of the service revolution of making your business customer-driven requires a re-examination of traditional structures. Traditionally, organisations have looked like model (a) in Diagram 2.

This is a pattern based upon policies and decisions made 'on high', communicated down-the-line to low status representatives, who delivered the service or product to the customer. The model is hierarchical, one-way, formal, usually slow-moving and discouraging of dynamism or initiative. In these top-down organisations, staff are preoccupied with what their managers want done.

If the customer is to be 'boss' then the pyramid needs to be turned upside down (b).

The key players then become those who contact the customers and shape their impressions. For the customer these people – the waiters, the ticket clerks, the delivery person, the counter assistants – *are* the company. *They* shape the organisation's image and the customers'

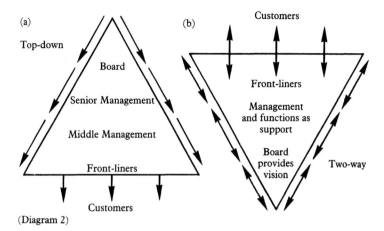

(Diagram 2)

perceptions of it. All management, all functions, actually exist only to make it easier for front-liners to please the customer, any other purpose is a distraction. The pyramid in this position needs to allow constant dialogue; customer to front-liners, front-liners to management and back again. In this kind of organisation, staff are preoccupied with what their customers want rather than what their manager wants. The need is for drive, skill, responsibility and initiative to be shaping every customer contact, to be making it easy for customers to do business with you and helping them to enjoy doing so. The task of management is to model in their contact with staff the standards of service, the quality of treatment and attention they want the customer to have.

If the task of the front-liner is to be a service hero, then the role of the manager is to be a service leader!

A total approach to success through service

If one is seeking a service revolution, where does one start? Success will require an integrated, sustained and total approach with these 5 elements:

Commitment from the top

Customer service initiatives are much more than training events. Training is one component in a total organisation approach to the pursuit of service excellence. The motivation of those taking part in that training is greatly enhanced by seeing that 'top people' are fully committed to the initiative and it is much more than 'flavour of the month'. There needs to be a very great emphasis on internal marketing of the service philosophy.

It is crucial to have all managers committed to a service initiative. The values underlying the programme need to be defined, communicated and modelled by the top team. It will often involve changes in the organisational structure to enable, for example, front-liners to have much greater authority to make decisions involving the customer. Unless all the managers are committed this can appear a threat to their authority. Line managers are key players whose task is to lead, market and model the service programme. Where management is not given a leading role, they can easily become blockers or saboteurs.

The company vision

Service training needs to be seen as flowing from the company's vision or mission. Knowing where the company sees its future, knowing what are its aspirations, its values, ambitions and targets, allows staff to see the purpose of and rationale for a quality service initiative.

Customer research

Quality service training promotes the idea that all business thinking starts with the customer. Who *are* our customers? What do they want/expect? These are questions staff need to be preoccupied with. The most successful businesses are in constant dialogue with their customers, seeking to learn about their needs and interests. Only regular provision of what the customer wants can bring success. Service companies need strategies for staying in touch with customer opinions. They also need to know what staff think. Staff know what are the blocks and barriers to service improvement and you must learn from them, involve them, and above all treat them with the same quality you want them to pass on to your customers.

Training

This component needs to promote the attitudes and skills which underpin excellence in customer service. It needs also to establish that the quality of service to external customers begins with the quality of service people, or departments provide to each other in-house. Its overall purpose is to produce the energy and the know-how to deliver excellence in 'managing the customer's experience'.

Follow-through
Generating the energy and skills which will promote customer service excellence produces a need to harness, manage, and channel what the training produces. A very key feature of any initiative needs to be strategies and systems for ensuring follow-through. Unless the product of the training can be applied, rewarded, reviewed and monitored then its full potential may not be realised.

Introducing a Service Initiative

The guidelines for achieving this successfully are no different to those which apply to the introduction of any major strategic changes. We particularly like the guidelines drawn up by Bob Nelson of the BBC who, coincidentally, has 12 of them.

12 RULES FOR CULTURE CHANGE

1. Clarity
Be absolutely clear about what (e.g. structure, systems, strategy) you want to change and why. Make it clear by when and how. Express it simply in words (e.g. competitive threat, cost escalation) which everyone can understand. Make it come alive! Use metaphors, symbols, slogans and pictures. Don't confuse the message, but create a picture or vision of how things will be after the change.

2. Consistency
Stick to it! Don't introduce inconsistency. It will take time if it's a major change. The turnaround in Jaguar's quality took three years, British Airway's culture change took five years and Citicorp's new market position took three years.

3. Context
Set the change in its proper context. No one ever starts with a clean slate! Connect what you want to achieve with other things that others want to achieve. 'Position' it properly (i.e. which bits of what we've got now fit the new order?).

4. Colleagues

No one ever changed an organisation alone! Enlist the support of colleagues to take action and make the change happen. Lone 'hero innovators' are usually martyred!

5. Champion

Get a real champion or champions of the idea. People whom others will follow are good champions. People in positions of status or power can be useful too! People with energy who can earn the professional respect of others are ideal. They need to be able to cope with ambiguity, uncertainty and complexity; change is not easy.

6. Communication

Tell everyone about it! Plan communications carefully. Publicise success stories. Create myths and stories which are positive. Mobilise pieces of 'theatre' to get the message across. Use every medium at your disposal. Work the grapevine and deal directly with rumours.

7. Commitment

Don't embark on it unless people at the top are really prepared to commit themselves to the change – psychologically, physically and intellectually. It really has to matter to them (or a single person at the top). Someone, somewhere positively has to want to change! Transformational leaders (e.g. Iacocca of Chrysler, Welch of General Electric, Egan of Jaguar, Marshall of British Airways and Harvey-Jones of ICI) believed in what they were doing and worked harder than anyone else to achieve it. They had vision and a passion for excellence.

8. Celebration

Find every excuse to celebrate small successes. Make the process of change fun so that others will want to join and help. It's often lonely! Celebrations are good ways of supporting those in the firing line, and helping them to cope.

9. Coalitions

Build coalitions with other groups, departments who may want the same change – but maybe for different reasons. Work at it together. Get a critical mass working for the change as soon as you can.

10. Consequences

Spot the consequences and knock-on effects of your change early. Change in one part of a system often unsettles a remote and unintended part. For example if you're changing the organisational structure – what happens to the business systems, the culture and strategy? Watch the consequences carefully!

11. Cement

Cement the change into the fabric of the organisation. Make it a normal part of life. Institutionalise it then move on. Disband the *ad hoc* arrangements set up to implement the change.

12. Courage

The courage of the leader or top team to drive the initiative through. The distinction is made here between transformational leadership – dedicated to a values driven fundamental change, and transactional leadership – in which the daily transactions of the business are well managed but subject to blowing with the corporate wind.

Profit through people

Some organisations have seen their priorities and business philosophy in this order:

profit
product
people

The pursuit of profit dominated all thinking, all policies and all management of people. The product was the chief source of profit so it was next in importance. People came at the bottom of the scale because their only relevance and value was in terms of the other two. In service organisations the model needs to be:

people
product
profit

People, especially those who manage the customer's experience, are key assets. Develop them, encourage, inspire and support them and they will deliver the service excellence, the quality product, which will make you profitable. Investment in people is a central quality service requirement, it is not optional!

Win/win/win

Customer service training equips people to add value to the products they sell. It establishes that one has the potential to 'develop relationships' with customers and not just sell products. It starts from a belief that 'you don't have to be ill to get better'. It does not start from a critical stance about the past and the present. It encourages people to become more aware and more skilled so that it occurs to them that they can do more and be more to enhance their jobs, their business and the customer's experience. Service training aims at

Win/Win/Win

outcomes. The customer wins because everyone likes quality treatment. The member of staff wins because everyone gets more satisfaction from a job well done. The business wins because the evidence shows that people return for quality attention and also advertise it to others.

And win?

And maybe there is a fourth winner – society! If quality treatment of people is to become the great concern of the business world, if it can be re-emphasised in the 'caring professions', in our education systems, in health and community services, in political movements, then there really must be hope for greater quality of life for us all.

Any organisation which wishes to contribute to that service revolution can find a formula for success in the 12 steps described in the remainder of this book. We wish you adventure and reward as you take them.

STEP 1

DECIDE ON YOUR CORE BUSINESS

We can be one of the best or one of the rest

> 'One of the most important things an
> organisation can do is to determine
> what business it is in.'
>
> Peter Drucker

Do you really know what business you're in?

Does this question sound naive? If it does, it shouldn't! Service excellence requires great clarity of business purpose.

Ask anyone with long experience in an organisation 'What business are you in?' and they are likely to perceive it as some sort of trick question. The way the question is answered, however, will decide all sorts of things about the way a business operates, what its priorities are, who its competitors are, and what it needs to do to better them. Let's illustrate this by comparing answers given in different businesses:

By house managers from different pubs in a brewery chain: 'We're in the business of selling beer. Our customers want a good pint that's not too expensive.'

'We're in the leisure business. Our customers want a good night out, with entertainment, good food and drink available.'

By branch managers in a building society: 'We're in the business of providing home loans and savings accounts.'

'We're in the business of providing financial services to people, helping them with savings, investments, insurance cover, loans including mortgages, and general money management.'

By airline employees: 'We're in the flying business, getting people from A to B, safely and quickly.'

'We're in the travel business, making it easy and pleasurable for people to spend time in different parts of the world as they work or holiday.'

By coaches in a sport and leisure club: 'Our business is to produce future top sports performers and champions. Our job is to spot the youngsters with most potential and provide them with our best attention and facilities to help them progress.'

'We are in the business of providing enjoyment in games and sport for families and people generally in our community. Sport for all is our business.'

Each answer given indicates different perceptions of their business which will lead to very different attitudes and approaches. The way you perceive your business will decide your business priorities, your marketing strategies, how you train your staff, develop your product range and build your business. If you believe you're in the business of selling a car to a customer you will run your business differently from somebody who wants the customer to return regularly each time s/he changes their car over a lifetime.

Organisations periodically need to revisit the question. You may be certain about what your core business is, but does everyone else see it that way? And do your customers see it your way?

The nature of your core business may actually change, subtly or even dramatically. Peters and Waterman in their best selling book *In Search of Excellence,** talk about the importance of 'sticking to your knitting'. This is good advice – but only to a point. If the majority of Swiss watchmakers had rigidly stuck to their knitting they would mostly now be out of business. Japanese digital watches were more reliable, trouble-free and cheap. The Swiss had previously regarded their core business as producing small machines that tell the time accurately and that lasted a lifetime. The Japanese and the microchip combined did this better.

The Swiss then really began to pay attention to what customers wanted, and two separate businesses began to emerge.

There was a limit as to how special and different a digital watch could be made; put an alarm on it, add a stop-watch function, a calculator, even a personal databank (with the watches looking increasingly bulky and almost requiring a technical diploma before you knew how to operate them!). There was a period when digital watches were special but mass production soon removed that image.

---

* Tom Peters and Robert Waterman, *In Search of Excellence*, Harper & Row, 1982.

There are always people with money who want to purchase items that they believe communicate clearly to other people that they have both money and good taste. This was illustrated in the world of denim jeans. Designer jeans with expensive labels found a market with this affluent group. People happily paid three or four times the price of ordinary jeans just to be able to differentiate themselves from the denimed masses.

Instead, therefore, of trying to combat the Japanese by producing even cheaper watches, some of the Swiss manufacturers went deliberately up-market. They redefined their core business from that of producing excellent crafted machines that were accurate time-keepers to that of producing *expensive wrist jewellery*. To emphasise the point, many of these watches dispensed with numbers altogether, making it almost impossible to read the time accurately. In other words, they were removed as far as possible from a computer style read-out of 18.32 and 41 seconds. This degree of accuracy was, by implication, required only by artisans who by necessity had to watch the clock. The leisured, rich classes had no similar imperative.

The makers of cheaper Swiss watches who did not have the 'names' nor the craftspeople to produce expensive wrist jewellery looked hard at the Japanese watches and saw that although technically superb, from a design standpoint they were boring. Either black or chrome with square or rectangular bodies and matching watch straps, it was difficult to distinguish one from another. So they too entered the wrist jewellery department, but not aimed at the Gucchi, Porsche and Piaget group, but at the youngsters for whom digital watches were the norm. This group took accuracy for granted and were used to seeing digital time everywhere – public clocks in stores and stations, videotext, computers, clock-radios, etc. The result was the Swatch watch and its various imitators (including, more recently, products from Japan and other Far Eastern countries). The core business here is providing *fashion accessories* at prices that mean that young people can own a selection of watches that are carefully chosen along with earrings, bracelets, necklaces and scarves before they begin their evening out. Some of the watches can be bought with a selection of different coloured wristbands and cases. The emphasis is on fun and design.

And in the Saturday markets of the UK's cities and towns throwaway digital watches can be bought for £1! Tom Peters quotes a banker friend of his who said, 'Niche or be niched'.

One core business has mushroomed into four quite different core businesses or niches. Yet they all could be described as being in the watch business.

The watch business

CORE BUSINESS

PRE-DIGITAL ERA	POST-DIGITAL ERA
1) Producing accurate time-keeping machines which last a lifetime.	1) Advanced digital watches for people who like or need to keep accurate time and require additional functions. 2) Cheap digital watches for people with little money to spend. 3) Expensive wrist jewellery. 4) Fashion accessories.

Are you still certain that you know what your core business is? And will it remain so?

Sir Hector Laing, chairman of United Biscuits, said recently, 'I used to think I was in the biscuit business. Then in 1964, I thought I was in the long-life convenience foods business. By 1972 I had come to the conclusion we were in the stomach business'.

Let us look at some examples of how core businesses have changed:

The British pub

It might be supposed that the core business here is to provide alcohol for people to drink.

For many pubs in the past this was largely the case. People went to them to drink to get drunk. They were sparsely furnished with sawdust on the floor, to make it easier to sweep up cigarettes, spilt drinks and even more unmentionable things. Yet there will be few publicans in business today who still think that their core business is to help people to get drunk – cheaply. The core business now is entertainment.

A modern pub manager needs to think about what kind of entertainment will be on offer. Some of the contemporary alternatives include:

Family entertainment: Children's play area, computer games, video machines, juke box, family eating room

Business pub: Many tables, quick bar food, restaurant attached, little or no music, no games machines

Young professionals: Cocktails, hors-d'oeuvres, subdued lighting, possibly a restaurant attached with good quality and medium-priced food, music, coffee and mineral waters

Community pub: Team sports – darts, snooker, even rugby or cricket, special events and outings, personalised tankards for regulars, live music nights, cheap snacks

Wine bar: Eating area, good moderately priced food, large wine selection, lots of bar stools, lively pre-recorded music, no games machines

It's not sufficient any more just to want to run a pub! You need to be clear exactly what kind of pub business you will be in, and which customers you are designing your business for.

Professional cricket

In the 1950s and early 1960s cricket was dying as a spectator sport. Fewer people had lifestyles that enabled them to attend three-day matches. Young people were growing up and finding the game something that belonged to a bygone era. The professional one-day game was developed and brought thousands of people back into cricket and many thousands more to the game for the first time. They experienced Sunday league, knockout competitions, international all-rounder competitions with top players to be seen in multicoloured gear and playing to very strange rules. Crowds loved it, though the enthusiasm was often not shared by the followers of the traditional game.

But what professional cricket has done is to create a core business of family entertainment which will help financially to keep its traditional 'business' in existence.

The rapid growth of indoor cricket, first in Australia and now in Britain, is an excellent example of how a core business can change. Indoor cricket has been designed more for playing than watching. It is a game for both sexes, allowing a wide range of abilities. It is brief (about 1½ hours), helps people keep fit, and is ideally suited to work and social groups playing for fun or for competition. But it definitely *isn't cricket!*

Scandinavian Airlines (SAS)

'The future belongs to people who see possibilities before they become obvious.'
Theodore Levitt

When Jan Carlzon took over SAS he found that the airline was trying to be in every kind of airline business – charter flights, special trips, holidays, business travel, cargo. After an analysis of where the income was generated, Carlzon redefined the core business of SAS as that of being a business person's airline. From then on all activity would be centered on making SAS the 'best business airline in Europe'.

Developing that clarity of focus allowed SAS to target all its efforts in that specialist direction. The belief that any business can be all things to all people paves the road to bankruptcy.

Porsche cars

The core business of motor car manufacturers is to provide vehicles that people can drive to get from A to B. Or is it? All motor cars can do that. But some manufacturers are selling something other than moving vehicles. Porsche, and their advertising make this perfectly clear, are selling status and style first and motor cars second. Of course, their product is excellent, but then there are many other excellent cars available at much lower prices.

The status and style begins from the moment you purchase the car – no discounts, often a waiting list, preferred no trade-in policy (unless another Porsche). The customer service areas are expensively and tastefully designed, with Porsche-designed goods available: very expensive leisure clothes, sunglasses, luggage, sports gear, etc. There are no 'secondhand' Porsches, only 'pre-owned'. After a service the car is completely valeted and no money changes hands. Accounts are sent.

When you buy a Porsche you don't just buy a car, you buy a badge which communicates information to the world about your lifestyle and success.

Bang & Olufson

They make hi-fi equipment and televisons don't they?

No, they do not. They make very expensive, luxury electronic furniture. The sound and vision production is excellent but there are others which are as good. Their core business is to produce stylish furniture which also provides quality sound and vision. They describe it as 'selling a lifestyle'.

Quality is remembered long after price is forgotten.

Volvo Concessionaires

Volvo make their core business very clear; it is to offer 'to an identified customer group, a total ownership experience which is second to none'. They are not interested in the market which responds to large discounts and price cuts. John Metcalfe, their Customer Service Director, says that 'if that is your business, people remember you only for your last discount. We sell total service – it's the experience people get when they go to their dealer which counts'. Volvo clearly do not pitch for the same market as Porsche, Lotus or Jaguar. Their reputation was built on safety, reliability and durability and not on speed, acceleration and designer styling. 'A Volvo must always handle the way the driver expects. Excitement is for the racetrack.' The emphasis is on aftersales service, added value, and lifetime care.

How do you decide what is your core business?

Success requires that you know exactly what business you are in. To become clear:

- ask yourself
- ask your colleagues
- ask your bosses
- ask your staff
- ask your customers
- ask your competitors.

Throughout this book we are continually emphasising the importance of research in developing success through service. Stay close to your customer, stay close to your staff. Listen upwards, outwards, listen downwards. Listen to your competitors. They may not be totally open or honest or even forthcoming but they *will* have an image of your organisation. What is it?

Do you have a core business within the core business?

Perhaps your department is finance, or marketing, or production, or sales, or computer services? As well as your organisation having its own core business, each department or section will, similarly, have its own core business. What's yours? Whatever it is, you should know how it relates to the organisation's core business.

SERVICE POINTERS

The following examples are based on actual experiences. Their aim is to show you just what good service means by focusing on specific situations. Such examples occur at the end of each step.

'I booked a table in a wine bar/restaurant for 12 people at the beginning of the Christmas period. I had been a regular visitor to the establishment.

'Three days ahead I phoned, spoke to the patron (whom I knew well and him me) and asked him to increase our booking by 4 people to 16. He sounded busy but said that it would be quite in order and he looked forward to seeing us later that week.

'When we arrived at the restaurant (on time) the place had been set for only 12. The manager came over on seeing that a larger group had gathered around a smaller table. I reminded him of our earlier conversation and assumed that an oversight had been made.

'To my amazement and embarrassment he denied to the entire group that he held a booking for 16. He said that I had not phoned him that week and that I must have been mistaken. Fortunately, my husband had overheard me speaking to him and suggested that *he* could have been mistaken.

'He continued that he had received no such phone call and that our booking was for 12 people. The restaurant was full and we asked him to offer a suggestion to resolve the matter – he said there was nothing he could do.

'At such a time we knew that there was nowhere else to go and be sure of being accommodated. So my husband and I and another couple waited in the bar area whilst 12 of our friends sat down to "enjoy" their evening. Later, much later, we were able to join them.

'Towards the end of the evening I sought out the manager/owner in private and explained to him that I would not be visiting his establishment again. He admitted that he may have been "hasty" but thought that I was being "unreasonable" as it was his busiest evening and I should make allowances.

'I have not visited this restaurant again and have related the episode to a number of people – and so have my friends.'

- **The patron could have turned this problem into a situation which would have won him customers for life. How?**
- **Do you always turn difficulties to your advantage?**

'Over Easter we visited two restaurants in the same week. Neither was particularly busy.

'The first was an establishment with a very high reputation and the food was good. The maitre d' was reasonably efficient but totally unwelcoming – he did not smile, made no eye contact, made no attempt at even casual conversation. He gave the same treatment to other diners, and we heard people on another table refer to him as "Happy Harry". Even though the other staff tried hard, the maitre d' had got the evening off to a bad start. We vowed not to return.

'In the following week we visited the Light of Bengal restaurant in Oldham. We had been there just twice before. The restaurant was busy but certainly not full. We were welcomed with a smile and recognition even though our previous visit was three months before. A friendly, and efficient, waitress took our order and bade us "Enjoy your meal" when she brought the food.

'During the meal, an extra dish appeared and the waitress explained that it did not presently appear on the menu but it was planned to have it included – she explained that the manager wished us to try it, and give him our opinion after the meal.

'When we had eaten we were invited to join the manager for liqueurs – he brought them to our table and asked for our thoughts on the new dish.

'We had gone with friends who had never previously visited that restaurant – they now go every month!'

- **Do you do anything to make your regular customers feel special?**
- **What more could you do?**

STEP 2

KNOW YOUR CUSTOMERS – AND YOUR COMPETITORS!

The only real measure of business success is a satisfied customer, all else is a distraction.

Your company's greatest assets are your customers.
Do you know *who* your customers really are?
When did you last try to find out?
What techniques did you use?
Do you know what they expect from you?
Are you and your staff in regular contact with your customers?
How do you utilise those contacts?

Perhaps you don't see any customers. Perhaps you work in an office and never see or talk to one. Perhaps you are on a shop floor where no customer dares to tread.

Wrong!

Everyone in an organisation has customers. If you do not have external customers you will have many internal customers. Step 5 will discuss how crucial it is *within* an organisation for people to give good service to one another.

This particular step is primarily concerned, however, with external customers. Having said that, as a person who works for the business you are always in a position of meeting actual or potential customers away from work and on site. How well do you represent your organisation?

The answer to that will depend largely on how it treats you within the everyday operations of the business, and how it represents you to the outside world. 'Who are your customers?' seems to be a question so simple as to be insulting to most people in business. 'Anybody who wants to buy what we provide' is the quick answer. But the skilful reply is not the quick one. There should be a measure of discernment in the successful business identifying carefully whom you wish to serve. Trying to be all things to all people is a business strategy with no future. Identifying market niches and selling to them is what business increasingly is about today.

Remember the SAS example in Step 1. The pub example too showed just how important it is to identify your target group. The jargon term is 'market segmentation', and you may have more than one segment. But be wary of having too many. Few businesses have made a success by trying to appeal to everyone.

As well as knowing who your customers are you also need to know what they expect. From the introduction Back to Basics, you will recall that:

**Good service is giving the
customers a little more
than they expect.**

That will not be possible until you know what they expect in the first place.

When we go to a hotel, we know what we expect: friendly reception, no problems with the reservation, a room well decorated, quiet, secure, with a comfortable bed, a telephone and TV that work, clean bedlinen, a clean bathroom with sufficient towels, toilet paper and lighting. That we expect. However, we do not expect to get, as we, the authors, did in the Westin Hotel in Calgary, Canada, a handwritten note from the concierge welcoming us, wishing us a pleasant stay, and giving us her telephone extension if we had any problems. We also do not expect what happened to one of our consultants on a repeat stay at the Penta Hotel at Heathrow – a card in his room saying, 'Welcome back, Mr Dodds'.

Simple, inexpensive, not over-the-top, but definitely a little more than we expected. Also, note that we are now giving free publicity to the Westin and Penta Hotels, and that is why good service leads to success. People pass on the good news.

They also pass on the bad news, often with even more relish, but more of that in Step 7. Let us look at how one major company tackled the question, 'Who are our customers and what do they want?'

British Airways*

In 1983 when Sir Colin Marshall and Lord King were given the task of preparing BA for privatisation they were faced with an airline in

---

* We are grateful to British Airways for allowing us to discuss their research findings so openly, and to Mike Bruce, a senior management development executive, who had a major charge to improve the quality of customer service in the airline.

Good service is not smiling at the customer but getting the customer to smile at you.

trouble: huge debts, a bureaucratic culture that had developed from government ownership, managers unused to taking risks, staff unused to finding out what the customers wanted.

When airline staff are asked what the customer wants they usually come up with factors like safety, good timekeeping, baggage arriving safely, good food, friendly service.

This is true, but this is what the customers *expect*. We all take this for granted when we plan a flying trip.

When BA asked their customers what they wanted they mentioned none of these things as priorities. When it came to gaining positive goodwill, or to use our terminology, *giving people a little bit more than they expect*, the customer wanted:

- To see mistakes and difficulties dealt with well, with sensitivity, concern and, where appropriate, humour; these might be delays, bad weather, running out of food, drink or duty-free items. Customers want staff to be good problem-solvers.
- To see staff showing and demonstrating caring concern for others less fortunate or more vulnerable than themselves – people with disabilities, the anxious, old people, children. The researchers discovered that there was a vicarious satisfaction in seeing caring demonstrated to others even if not required personally. It was an unspoken reassurance to every passenger. Interestingly, it was the supposedly hardbitten businessman more than any others who described the greatest satisfaction in seeing children being taken care of, given presents, etc.
- To be welcomed, to be treated as individuals, to have names used, to be wished 'a good trip' or 'a good holiday', even if it was recognised as a bit automatic, like the American 'have a nice day'. To quote directly from the research:

'There appears to be an almost magical value in a good wish quite out of proportion to its face value. When the staff are there and visible, giving a touch of personal contact, the experience is lifted out of the machine and system dominated routine and the passenger is less likely to feel submerged in a faceless mindless crush.'

- Unsolicited giving from the staff: sitting next to a passenger and chatting, spontaneous talking, unscheduled pilot comments, appearance of the captain.
- To get factual information. Why was there turbulence? How long might it last? Why the delay in taking off? Why is the plane circling? News about connections, whether the drinks are free and what movie will be shown.

Overall the researchers found that human relations with passengers were twice as important as any operational factors. They also found that bad experiences destroy goodwill more than positive ones add to it.

Customise, don't standardise!

Perhaps the single outstanding finding was that passengers did not want standardised treatment. They wanted the staff to be professional, courteous, but to be themselves – people in their own right, who dealt with them, the passengers, as individuals and not as pieces of human cargo to be transported from A to B.

This research demonstrates that it is crucial to tap the knowledge held by staff about your customers but there is no substitute for asking the customers themselves. Methods for doing this are described in Step 8.

As well as knowing its customers exceedingly well, a sophisticated service operation will also know its competitors; not simply knowing who they are, but knowing also their strengths and differentiators. If you are serious about being your customers' best choice, you must ask yourself:

- Who else is in the same core business?
- What do customers get from them that is different or better?
- What do we offer our customers that is different or better?
- What can we learn from the competition and how can we use that learning?
- How can we systematically keep in touch with our competitors as their service quality developers?

You can, in fact, learn a great deal by becoming a customer of the competition or asking your own staff members to do this. Be assured that if you are successful yourself, your competitors will be queuing up to learn from you! That is why quality service is a story of continuous improvement, you can never rest on your laurels.

'The journey to excellence is a journey not a destination.'

Mike Robson

Top service companies invest heavily in 'Benchmarking'. This moves beyond keeping a close eye on the competition. Somebody in one company explained to us:

'Two nags in the knacker's yard can pride themselves on being in better condition than each other, but they stay in the knacker's yard!'

> *Business is a lot like tennis – those who don't serve well end up losing.*

Benchmarking means asking who are the best in a particular area of expertise, and learning from them, though they may not be direct competitors of yours. This approach can help you make quantum leaps over your competitors, at least for a while, because they will be watching. Of course, you can ignore all this and sail blithely on: survival is not mandatory!

SERVICE POINTERS

The plumbing supplies showroom was about to close for the weekend. A breathless customer arrived just as the security man was about to lock up. 'Just wanted a replacement for this washer to repair a leaking toilet, but I suppose you are all closed down.' 'Come in, madam, the stores have closed, but let's see what we can do.' The security man looked at the washer, and inspected several of the showroom display units before finding one that seemed to be what he was looking for. He reached inside and dismantled some of the fittings. He returned to the customer proudly bearing one replacement washer. 'I'll ask the stores people to re-assemble that on Monday morning. Hope that you get your job fixed, madam.' 'That's great,' said a very grateful customer, 'How much?' 'No charge, madam, the tills are closed. Good luck!'

● **Is everybody connected with your business able to take initiatives on the customers' behalf?**

'I ordered a new fireplace which I was promised would be installed within three days to coincide with my decorating. The correct pieces failed to arrive so the installation was held up. When it arrived it wasn't quite the same as the one in the showroom but I accepted it in the interests of getting the job done. When it was finished it was ten days late. Then I got a bill saying it would cost more than I had agreed because the materials were better than the ones on display in the showroom! Two of my friends in the street have bought fireplaces since then but after my experience neither of them went to that company.'

● **What can we learn about service from that experience?**

STEP 3

CREATE YOUR VISION

The best vision is within sight but just out of reach

Three men were working. Each one was busy with a trowel, cement and bricks. A passer-by went up to the first one, who looked very bored, and asked him what he was doing. 'I'm laying bricks,' he replied sullenly. The passer-by then asked the second man, who looked somewhat more enthusiastic, the same question. 'I'm building a wall,' he replied. The third man was in high spirits, whistling as he worked, and seemed reluctant to be interrupted. When asked the same question, he replied proudly, 'I'm building a cathedral.'

Why are you in business? What makes you feel good? What gives you a spiritual high?

We all need a purpose, a vision, a mission—call it what you like—to motivate us to action. In organisations money rarely totally motivates people. A lack of it can create bad feeling and a lack of motivation; sufficient or even excess money will ensure that people are content but it will never fire their bellies or their imaginations. For that people need a purpose or a vision for which they are working.

We all need our cathedrals

The US space body, NASA, gives one of the best examples of the motivational power of a vision.

President Kennedy in 1960 provided NASA with a very clear vision:

'We will put a man on the moon by the end of the decade'.

This fits the two essential criteria for a powerful vision statement:

1) It should be able to be summarised in one line.
2) The goal should be within sight but just out of reach.

And, of course, that is exactly what happened at NASA. They made the target with six months to go. But what happened afterwards is equally instructive. Over the next two years, senior managers were admitting, unofficially, that productivity had dropped by about thirty per cent. There was now no target to aim for, no vision to inspire them, because the vision was never replaced.

One of the aphorisms we use on our Success Through Service programmes is that:

**People will march for a sentence
but never for a paragraph.**

To take three examples:

Liberty! Equality! Fraternity!

We will overcome!

Workers of the world unite!

These were all one-liners that dramatically changed history. Clearly a vision *is* a rallying cry. It empowers people. It makes them believe that they *can* do it.

A similar experience was noted at a certain UK engineering company at the time of the Falklands war. The QE2 had to be fitted with a helideck, a task that the management would have expected to take two weeks. It was completed in two days! And, as with the NASA example, within months of the war being over, productivity returned to normal.

These are the ways some UK companies summarise their vision for their people:

'To be the best provider of housing financial services in the UK!'
The Leeds

'We aim to build profitably the highest-quality car sold in Europe.'
Nissan UK

'Excellence and value in meeting personal financial needs.'
Abbey National

Organisations need to create a vision and embark on a process by which they get the commitment of their staff to that vision, so that they are effective as well as efficient.

An important distinction is sometimes made between efficiency and effectiveness.

a) Efficiency

b) Effectiveness

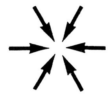

(Diagram 3)

Diagram 3a shows six departments, each of which is efficient. However, they are working to different ends. 3b shows what it looks like when the six departments are all working to the same end.

An *efficient* sales department makes many sales. An *effective* sales department makes sales consistent with production's capacity and feeds back important customer information to the production and marketing and accounting departments.

Recent research into what are the key elements in achieving a change to a quality service culture shows how vital it is to have a motivating, unifying vision. To have one, and nothing else, will achieve very little. To introduce training, research or motivational campaigns without a strong central business vision is also likely to be a poor investment.

Creating the vision

What should an effective vision statement look like? Although ideally it should always be possible to encapsulate it in one line, it will need initially to be much more comprehensive. The full statement should be made available to everyone, but the one-liner should be permanently visible about the premises.

A vision statement has many purposes. It:

- provides the visible evidence of the organisation's priorities and commitment;

- 'lights the flame' to launch initiative and remains a visible reminder as it unfolds;

- is the clarion call which gathers the troops and focuses on the task ahead;

- is the map of 'the promised land' which gives the people's journey a destination;

- is the measure by which the business says it would like to be judged;

- excites, inspires and concentrates the corporate mind.

A service mission statement establishes the vision to which the organisation should aspire.

It speaks stirringly: 'Service excellence is to be the beginning and end of all our efforts . . . we exist only to serve our customers and in that we wish to be the best in our business . . . we want our customers to have pleasure and benefit from their contact with us and our staff to take pride in being the best . . . we wish to be famous for our efficiency and our customer concern . . . to be profitable because we have enthusiastic and able staff dedicated to making our customers' interests and satisfaction their preoccupation . . . the customer is the most important person in our business, the one who gives us our jobs . . . the customer compliments us with her attention and deserves the most courteous treatment we can give her . . . we can provide the service excellence our customer deserves only through total teamwork and service to each other. . . .'

Such statements leave no doubt in the minds of staff or customers about the nature of the task. Making the mission so public raises the stakes. It carries high risk if delivery falls short, but its purpose is to leave no doubt as to the business priorities and expectations. It summons the troops but it does not in itself equip them for the fray.

It always states 'why' the organisation exists and does not dwell on 'what' will result – such as profits.

Below are some examples of the full company vision or mission statements:

The British Airways mission

- British Airways will have a corporate charisma such that everyone working for it will take pride in the company and see themselves as representing a highly successful world-wide organisation.

- BA will be a creative enterprise, caring about its people and its customers.

- We will develop the kind of business capability which will make BA the envy of its competitors, to the enhancement of its stockholders.

- British Airways will be a formidable contender in all the fields it enters, as well as demonstrating a resourceful and flexible ability to earn high profits wherever it chooses to focus.

- We will be seen as *the* training ground for talented people in the field of service industries.

- Whether in transport or in any of the travel or tourism activity areas, the term 'BA' will be the ultimate symbol of creativity, value, service and quality.

Our goals are to be
- The best and most successful in the fields of travel, tourism and transport.

- Known as the most efficient, the most customer-concerned as well as the safest at whatever it does.

- Able to ensure that the term 'BA Manager' is synonymous with people-concern, high achievement and general business capability.

- Maintaining constantly improving targets as a good employer as well as manifesting concerns for social and community opportunities and environmental standards wherever the company operates.

- Achieving a level of Return on Investment so that any shareholder will value his/her involvement with British Airways, and see it as an important and sound investment.

This is a vision designed for an organisation of 40,000 people.

The Body Shop

'We produce products that cleanse, polish and protect skin and hair. How we produce them and how we market them is what is interesting about us. We are innovative, we are passionate and we care. We are innovative in our formulations; we are passionate about environmental issues; we care about retailing. The image, goals and values of our company are as important as our products. Our mission is to be the most honest cosmetic company around.'

The mission statement that Anita Roddick likes to use is a quote by Mahatma Gandhi that she saw pinned on the wall in a bank on her travels in India:

'A customer is the most important visitor on our premises. He is not dependent on us. We are dependent on him. He is not an interruption on our work. He is the purpose of it. He is not an outsider in our business. He is part of it. We are not doing him a favour by serving him. He is doing us a favour by giving us an opportunity to do so.'

This is the vision for over 3,000 central and franchised staff.

Digital Equipment Company

MISSION: To be recognised as the best provider of quality integrated information systems, networks and services to support customers worldwide.
What does the mission statement mean?

Be recognised – We want to be the best and have our customers know it.

The best provider – We are a reliable and easy-to-do-business-with international supplier.

Quality – Measured by customer satisfaction and adherence to the highest standards in the industry.

Integrated information systems and networks—The way in which a company acquires, shares, integrates and uses data to fulfil its mission, optimise its productivity and competitiveness and plan its evolution. This includes a wide range of compatible information-handling products suitable for a heterogeneous multi-vendor environment, from

Vision takes you from the past and commits you to the future.

the user-tuned workstation to non-stop multi-MIP computers, supported by a complete set of software tools, applications and consultancy, integrated with internal and external networks and database architectures.

Services – The widest range of services from first contact through end of product life and any services with added value to help the customer to design, implement and manage her information systems and networks, setting the effectiveness standard in the industry and continuing to set the pace in service technology.

Customers worldwide – From the individual professional to the large multinational enterprise in all its locations.

Lifeskills

Below is our own vision for Lifeskills, a company employing around 30 people. We reproduce this not for vanity's sake but to demonstrate that this is as important for small companies as for large ones.

'We wish to be an exceptional organisation making a unique and special contribution to business, education and the community.

'We seek to be the best in promoting self-empowerment in individuals and organisations by developing excellence in:

- training concepts, materials and programmes;

- educational materials for young people and adults;

- projects which promote self-management;

- consultancy which can respond most skilfully to our customers' needs.

'We will be a business with:

- local

- national

- and international focus.

'We will increase our profitability each year in order to expand our work, finance new initiatives, create job opportunities and benefit all staff.

'We will be the kind of organisation the future will require. This means we will:

- promote interdependency, not dependency;

- be a 'can-do' culture, operating flexibly and fluidly in our structures and organisation style;

- encourage entrepreneurship, and the creation of new initiatives consistent with our goals and values;

- we will be committed totally to the personal, professional and organisational development of all involved with Lifeskills, either as customers of our services or as staff who provide those services. We will recognise that our customers come first, because without them nothing else is possible, but we will model in our work with each other, the quality of relationship and service we wish our customers to receive;

- we will be an organisation which models the values we promote in our training and publishing which is built on the purpose of **helping people to help themselves**;

- we will be effective in achieving these goals by working to clear objectives, explicit systems and unambiguous contracts;

- we will work for people, through people, with people, and create work, fun and profit in doing that;

- we will be an organisation in which there is **excitement, experiment, enjoyment and excellence.**'

Our one-liner is:

**Lifeskills: Making a difference
with style and integrity**

We are always impressed when we see a company's vision statement displayed to customers as well as to staff.

A Seattle based chain of clothing stores offers this example. The 'creed' as Eddie Bauer stores call it is always reproduced in large letters on a wall near the cash register:

**To give you such outstanding quality,
value, service and guarantee that we may
be worthy of your high esteem**

A vision is not a financial objective

Note that none of these visions refers to financial targets. This is because a financial target is an objective, not a vision. It is crucial as a yardstick and as a target, but people other than the board of directors and shareholders rarely get excited about achieving a turnover of £15 million or a pre-tax profit of £1.5 million.

A vision is not a plan

Visions and plans are mutually dependent. You cannot have one without the other. A vision without a plan remains a dream. A plan without a vision is a recipe for being busy – but towards what ultimate end?

Visions need to come first, plans afterwards.

The best visions are sensual

'We will develop technology sufficient to enable a direct investigation of the physical and biological constituents of our closest natural satellite, and we wish to achieve this capability within a framework of 10 years.'

'We will put a man on the moon by the end of the decade.'

Which of these will set the fire running through your veins?

They are both vision statements but the one is conceptual and the other sensual. With the second one you can see the picture, you can almost hear the bump as 'man' lands on the surface of the moon.

Recall Martin Luther King's 'I have a dream'. He did not simply talk about freedom, rights and equality. He painted word pictures so that his audience could see and feel them: he talked of his view from 'the mountain', he saw 'the promised land', he described black children and white children playing together.

His audience could see the pictures and feel their significance.

We are not suggesting that all senior managers attempt to emulate John F. Kennedy and Martin Luther King, but they do need to motivate through visions.

Look at this example from Cray Research UK, which really gives you a picture and a feel for what it would be like working for the company that produces the world's fastest computers.

The Cray style

'At Cray Research UK, we take what we do very seriously; but we don't take ourselves too seriously.

'There is a sense of pride at Cray. Professionalism is important. People are treated like and act like professionals. But people are professional without being stuffy.

'Cray people trust each other to do their jobs well and with the highest ethical standards. We take each other very seriously.

'We have a strong sense of quality – quality in our products and services, of course; but also quality in our working environment, in the people we work with, in the tools that we use to do our work, and in the components we choose to make what we make.

'Economy comes from high value, not from low cost. Aesthetics are part of quality. The effort to create quality extends to the communities in which we work and live as well.

'The Cray approach is informal and non-bureaucratic. Verbal communication is key, not memos. "Call, don't write" is the watchword.

'People are accessible at all levels.

'People also have fun working at Cray Research. There is laughing in the halls, as well as serious conversation. More than anything else, the organisation is personable and approachable; but still dedicated to getting the job done.

'With informality, however, there is also a sense of confidence. Cray people feel like they are on the winning side. They feel successful, and they are. It is this sense of confidence that generates the attitude of "go ahead and try it, we'll make it work".

'Cray people like taking responsibility for what they do and thinking for themselves. At the same time, they are proud to share a single mission – making the world's fastest computers.

'Because the individual is key at Cray, there is a real diversity in the view of what Cray Research really is. In fact, Cray Research is many things to many people. The consistency comes in providing these diverse people with the opportunity to fulfil themselves and experience achievement.

'The creativity, then, that emerges from the company comes from the many ideas of the individuals who are here. And that is the real strength of Cray Research.'

The steps to creating a vision

1) Top team

The top management team have first to decide on their own vision for the organisation.

> '*A vision is where you are going; a plan is how you get there.*'
> H. Woodward and S. Buchholz

They need to ask themselves three very important questions:

• Why are we in business?

• What do we want to achieve?

• How are we going to do it?

When we work as consultants to top teams this process typically takes place in comfortable, relaxing surroundings, well away from interruptions and visual reminders of tasks to be done. One company we worked with described this process as:

> 'Selecting our mountain to climb
> Ensuring it is the right one
> Checking why we want to climb it
> Working out what we need to do
> Deciding how we are going to do it
> And when we are going to start.'

How does a top team set about creating its vision?
We recommend a variety of techniques but one to get a team thinking in the right direction is as follows:

• Define five things we would like our customers to say about us.

• Define five things we would like our staff to say about us.

• Define five things we would like our competitors to say about us.

From this a team then begins to produce a concise but comprehensive vision statement, combining clarity with excitement, which ideally can always be encapsulated in one sentence.

Having created the vision at the top, the next step is to communicate this throughout the organisation and to get feedback.

In British Airways Sir Colin Marshall made a video which was shown to all departments. This explained the vision (or mission in their case) which was crafted by a senior management group working with him. The importance of this was made clear from what he learned by personally attending almost every one of the two-day service skills workshops which all 40,000 BA staff attended in groups of 180 at a time. He used to have a 30-minute, no holds barred question and answer session, and if he couldn't attend personally another director did. It is not surprising that he was soon perceived by the staff as a superhero after demonstrating that level of commitment.

2) Middle management

Middle management are the key to promoting and managing the vision.

The crucial 3 questions for them are:

- How can we contribute to this vision?

- How can we be models of it?

- How can we get our front-liners excited about it?

Although the vision must come from the top, in itself it is useless unless the middle managers feel they can own it, and preferably have an opportunity to contribute to it.

3) Front-liners

They are the deliverers. They, too, must have an opportunity to ask three crucial questions:

- How can we contribute to this vision?

- How does it relate to our customers?

- How do we make it happen?

The final vision

This will be one initiated and defined from the Top Team, listened to, digested and contributed to by middle management, discussed and contributed to by the front-liners who then implement it directly with the customers.

Sensitive organisations might even like to test it out on valued customers.

A strong central vision is the basis for empowering departments, functions and individuals within the organisation. Quality service requires everybody to take responsibility and ownership within the vision. The process then is:

Central Vision – decentralised responsibility!

The ultimate achievement

Everyone in the organisation should be able to describe and justify the vision, and will be able to say exactly how his or her work contributes to that vision.

'The ideal organisation, and the one with the best chance of success, is one where if you ask anyone, from the chairman down to the newest recruit on the shop floor, what the business is trying to do, you would get the same answer.'

John Harvey-Jones

The process is all-important

How the vision gets defined is perhaps even more important than the vision itself. Wise organisations will embark on a whole series of vision creation sessions. Each department needs its own statement and its one-liner relating to the overall vision and one-liner. For example, the key beliefs of the Allied Dunbar approach are defined as:

Commitment to service
Demanding and caring
Positive management

A booklet expanding on each of these is given to all staff. Each department then produces its own mission statement which links to the company statement. The administration section has four operating divisions and each of these is working on producing its own mission statement. The company mission statement has, in addition, been distributed to all policy holders.

Each person needs their own personal vision and needs to know how that can fit into the larger picture. One way of doing that is to offer opportunities for line management to help individuals identify their own personal visions. As part of performance or career reviews many organisations now offer this to their staff.

Customer service and mission

A recent report from Ernst & Whinney* covering 154 companies and organisations shows that 98% of them strongly agree that customer service should have its own mission statement. In practice only 70% have produced a written mission statement. Perhaps, not surprisingly, it is the larger companies which were more likely to have done this.

Interestingly enough, in most cases companies with a mission

* Customer Service, July 1988

The best vision is within sight but just out of reach.

statement appear to have achieved most in customer service – over 12% believe that their customer service programme meets all of its objectives, whereas none of the companies without a mission statement make this claim.

SERVICE POINTERS

Liz Clarke, our Training Director, had booked her VW GTI in to Massingberds in Harrogate for its 10,000 mile first service. She was greeted with a smile by the man on reception who looked at her and said, 'Good morning, Ms Clarke. You've brought your GTI in for service. I know that when you booked it in they would have asked if there was anything else you would like looking at but I'll just make sure by asking again.'

She hadn't said it the first time because it seemed so ridiculous but encouraged by the receptionist's approach she said, 'Well I am getting a strange *graunch* sound when I reverse up kerbs! – and come to think of it my Honda Prelude used to do that too.'

'Oh,' he said, 'You must be concerned about that, we'll have a good look at it.' He arranged a time for collection and for one of their cars to take her into Harrogate.

Back at the pick-up he greeted her with: 'We've got to the bottom of your "graunch", Ms Clarke. It's obviously an up-market noise. When you reverse up kerbs the front spoiler drags on the floor and makes a peculiar scraping sound.'

Much reassured she left thinking back to the time she had taken her previous car to a different garage and the man talking to a mechanic had glanced at her with a 'drop your keys in that basket' and hardly paid any attention to 'But I'd like to mention this "graunch".' He said, 'It's probably the suspension on these cars you're not used to.'

The car came back complete with "graunch". She felt uneasy about the car and soon after, she sold it. Next time she passed the garage there was a large For Sale notice outside.

- **Do you always really listen to the customer and treat her/him as an individual?**

- **Are you ever guilty of patronising your customers?**

STEP 4

DEFINE YOUR MOMENTS OF TRUTH

Good service is giving people a little more than they expect. Excellent service is enjoying giving people a little more than they expect.

SAS has 10 million passengers a year. The average passenger comes in contact with five SAS employees. Therefore SAS is the product of the 10 million times the five. SAS is fifty million Moments of Truth per year. Fifty million, unique, never to be repeated opportunities to distinguish ourselves in a memorable fashion, from each and every one of our competitors. My job is simply to "manage the dickens" out of the fifty million Moments of Truth. SAS is the contact of one person (the customer) in the market and one person at SAS. That is SAS.

Jan Carlzon

When do you make your decision that:

- this hotel is going to be good;
- this shop will provide you with good service;
- this product will be really good;
- this restaurant is one you will revisit;
- this dentist is going to be your regular one;
- this bank will offer you what you need;
- this airline is one you will fly with again?

These decisions are made as a direct result of your experiences with the organisation or its products. They are not usually made in a long thought-through analysis but through brief encounters with all the elements of service that we would label as the 'packaging' around the core business.

Jan Carlzon at SAS discovered that on average those 50 million moments of truth (points of contact between a customer and a SAS staff member) averaged between 15 to 30 seconds. Yet each of those moments contains the potential for the customer to experience feelings ranging from magical to nightmarish, passing through all points on the journey including indifference.

The phrase 'moments of truth' comes from the world of bullfighting and the corrida. It is that moment towards the end of the fight when the matador and the bull face each other eye to eye. Each of them has an instant to make a decision, and the outcome of the event is determined at that moment. Its use in a service context establishes just how crucial is every point of contact with the customer.

The service experience

Your business, whether it is in transport, manufacturing, publishing, selling insurance or banking services, etc, will contain many thousands of moments of truth between you and your customer. How you measure up at these moments will determine whether that customer a) *becomes* your customer, or b) *remains* your customer, and c) *brings new customers* to you by spreading the good news.

Any customer's experience of any business will be decided by what we call the '4 Ps'. It is a method for analysing the ways in which a business creates an experience for the customer. The customer's impression will be shaped by:

people skills
product
presentation
processes

To achieve success through service you need to *manage the customer's experience* of your business by ensuring that:

- all your staff or representatives have **excellent people skills;**

- you are selling or offering **superb products;**

- your **presentation** is impressive – of the product or service and its surroundings;

- the **processes** which deliver or support the product or service are customer centred.

The Body Shop

The Body Shop is an excellent example of a retail chain that pays close attention to managing their customers' experience.

Anita Roddick ensured from the beginning that her business would always be 'values driven'. She will not compromise on any of the beliefs that she had when she launched the business. As a result of this, any analysis of moments of truth for the Body Shop must begin with the public image that she has actively created. When people read or hear about the Body Shop they find that the company:

- never advertises;

- believes that it is immoral to think, 'how much can we get?' when they launch a new product, and instead has a fixed profit percentage;

- will never sell goods that have involved testing on animals;

- will only sell products made from natural ingredients;

- does not waste money on fancy packaging;

- sells refillable products;

- supports environmental protection and sponsors causes like Greenpeace, and will never use aerosols in their products.

So, your public image, in itself, is an accumulation of many moments of truth. This image can only be built up gradually yet, sadly, it can be destroyed rapidly.

If we analyse a customer's direct experience of a Body Shop in terms of 'moments of truth' and the '4 Ps' we find the following to be true:

Appearance of the shop externally (presentation)
The decision to enter a shop or not is often made in an instant. A Body Shop not only looks smart in its green and white colours, but the windows are beautifully dressed, inviting you to go in and look around further. In addition, a Body Shop anywhere in the world has its own unique smell which drifts outside of the shop and draws you in.

Immediate impact as you enter
(presentation)
Anita Roddick believes in retail as theatre. The colours and designs inside are carefully thought out, the lighting designed to enhance the products. The shop assistants are deliberately dressed to fit in with the culture and to look approachable, unlike some of the intimidating, over made-up, unsmiling (in case it breaks the mask) assistants one often encounters on cosmetic counters. The franchised shops are regularly visited by central Body Shop personnel, and the internal image is checked. The assistants must always look clean and healthy – no black nail varnish, for example. There are to be no sellotaped cards in the windows, messy handwritten signs, postcards on the wall – nothing, in fact, that is not in keeping with Body Shop philosophy and image.

The products are laid out for convenience to the shopper; for example, bath products are all together, hair products in the same stand, etc. The merchandise is on separate product 'islands' that make it easy for the customer to wander around.

The staff behaviour
(people skills)
The staff are not all lined up behind counters – the design of the shop would not permit this anyway. They are taught communication skills as part of an initial three months training scheme, during which time they will spend some time on courses at the Body Shop training centre, some time working in different shops, and some time on special projects.

There is no hard-sell to the customer. The staff are trained to give information to the customer and not simply to sell products.

As a customer you *should* be met by concerned, friendly, informative staff who clearly enjoy their work, are always busy but will always put *you* before stacking shelves, paperwork, refilling bottles, etc, who are prepared to talk to you as an individual, who do not have a plastic 'trained' approach, and who clearly have positive attitudes towards themselves and to customers.

Anita Roddick has the following statement on her office wall:

Our staff will have so much self-esteem about working in retail and it will be the very fact that they have worked in a Body Shop that gives credibility to their CV. We WILL have the best service in the country!

The products themselves
(product)
'The waiter who smiles will not make the steak taste better if it is bad meat, in fact, he may make it worse.'

In the Body Shop you will find a wide range of excellent products, all in a characteristic simple design (**presentation** again). All the major products are in five standard sizes making it easy to find the measure you want, and many of the bottles are refillable. The final moment of truth for any product, of course, is when you first use it, but until that particular moment you are encouraged to smell it, try it, touch it.

Buying the product
(people skills)
How are you treated at the till, especially if the assistants are under pressure? How is your money taken? Are you looked in the eye? Do you get a smile? Does the assistant say something to you? Does s/he respond when you say something? Are you wished goodbye as you leave? Body Shop staff have been trained to do these things well.

Returning to the shop
(people skills)
Are you remembered? Is the service still as good? Are you treated as an individual? If you want a refill are you treated as just as valuable a customer as if you were buying a new product?

If the experiences of ourselves, spouses, children and friends are anything to go by then you will find that the Body Shop capitalises on most, if not all, of its moments of truth. In every business moments of truth are to be studied and savoured. At those moments the total preoccupation needs to be:

• What does the customer want and expect?

• What can I do to provide that, and *that little bit more?*

• How can I leave the customer feeling good about the contact, good about me and good about the business?

Preoccupation with moments of truth is the key to service success. Quality service, however, requires more than a mechanically good performance at moments of truth. If good service is giving the customer a little more than s/he expects, then excellent service involves enthusiasm and enjoyment of doing so. Our earlier definition of service needs to be expanded because:

> EXCELLENT SERVICE
> =
> **ENJOYING** GIVING PEOPLE A
> LITTLE MORE THAN THEY EXPECT

> The best service companies have a
> passion for service excellence!

> Providers of service excellence
> do it with energy and enthusiasm!

> Excellent service is very much a
> WIN/WIN/WIN/WIN
> experience

The customer obviously wins by being on the receiving end of quality provision and attention.

The service provider wins because the customer's pleasure and satisfaction is reciprocated. The provider has the satisfaction of a job well done. Self-esteem and confidence are built by quality job performance.

The business wins because the quality of the service experience brings the customer back to buy again and, because most people talk about such experiences, they become living, walking advertisements which draw other people to the business.

Society also wins because customers leave feeling more positive about the world and themselves, and their next interpersonal encounters will be more positive, which in turn will be passed on, and so on . . .

A moment of truth has been well managed when the customer walks away feeling enriched and delighted by the experience.

Searching for the service opportunity
In today's competitive marketplace the customer decides who wins and who loses.

John Humphrey
CEO The Forum Corporation

Make it easy for your customers to do business with you.	Because of the customers' power, all staff at all levels need consciously to seek out opportunities for giving the customer that little bit more.

How do you deal with a customer who announces s/he is to become an ex-customer? With respect and gratitude? Look at how the Automobile Association responded to John Dodds, one of our consultants, when he withdrew membership.

Dear Mr Dodds

I am sorry to learn that you do not intend to continue your membership.

The Association owes a considerable debt of gratitude to members such as yourself, who have subscribed over many years in the past and it is with regret that I close your membership.

If your subscription has been paid by Bankers Mandate will you kindly ask your bank to ensure that this is cancelled, as they will not accept my instructions.

On behalf of the Association, I would like to thank you for your longstanding support.

John was impressed that they made no attempt to change his mind, and as a result it is clear that if he does decide to rejoin a motoring organisation he will choose the AA – 'all things being considered'.

'All things being considered' is a very important phrase. John will not rejoin the AA because of one well managed moment of truth. He will be asking himself:

Over the years how consistently good has their service been?

How does it compare in price and range of services offered with other motoring organisations?

Are their administrative practices user friendly?

But if all the motoring organisations are comparable on the 4 Ps, a well managed moment of truth could be all that it might take to win a customer. And once that customer is there, a service-oriented business *should not* lose them to a competitor.

Budget Rent-A-Car

In Chicago in 1987 the airport was closed as a result of an unusual autumn thunderstorm. The water was so deep on the airport access roads that ordinary cars could not get through. Taxis were having to drop their customers off in pouring rain hundreds of yards from their destinations. For Budget Rent-a-Car's courtesy-bus drivers whose vehicles could make it through the flooding, here was a moment of truth of which they could take advantage. For the duration of the storm, Budget drivers swept the airport access roads picking up every stranded passenger they could find, whether or not they were Budget customers.

'People remember things like that,' says Linda Rasins, Budget's director of training and development.

'This is a very competitive business and we try to instil in all our employees the idea that the way we treat customers is what will differentiate us in the marketplace. In this case, a little simple courtesy on the part of our drivers may well be the thing those people think about the next time they rent a car.'

Douglas Seaton, Yeovil

A customer calling to collect a serviced car at this Somerset Ford dealer finds a business card attached to the invoice bearing a photograph and the name of the 'technician' – the term 'mechanic' is no longer used – who worked on it, and offering a discussion of any problems.

Sogo Department Store, Tokyo

When you enter this huge store there are five or six receptionists in uniform, whose sole task is to welcome people. No one should enter without receiving a smile and a word of welcome. In each department, the *manager's* task is to welcome people to the department. There is a team briefing in each department each day before the doors open and the phrase that is used is that 'each day the doors open to let God in'. Staff are not allowed to talk to one another while customers are in the store, and at pressure times, all the staff-administrators, accounts people, managers, will work on the counters.

The mission statement is: 'There is nothing more important than serving the customer in this store.'

To give you some examples of positive moments of truth here is our gallery of service heroes and heroines, who gave us that little bit more:

Insurance

Peter Dean was a London Life salesman with whom we both had taken out single premium pension policies.

It was just before Christmas and there were 24 hours left to get all

*Whenever you
meet a customer
you ARE the
company.*

the documentation to our accountant to ensure that we received a sizeable tax allowance from the Inland Revenue for a half-yearly payment due on 1 January. As usual we looked helpless at the prospect of finding time at short notice to get to see our accountant and sort out details, as our accountant lives 70 miles from Leeds. Peter saw the problem, said that he would go early the next morning, see the accountant, sort out all the paperwork with him, and we need not give it another thought. A point to note here is that London Life do not pay commission to the sales staff. Not surprisingly, he got our next year's business too.

Restaurant

Esteban Vacas is one of the two owners of a restaurant called Los Charros in Moraira on the Costa Blanca, Spain. He is one of the best maitre d's that we have ever seen, unconsciously watching for cues to see whether a diner wishes to be talked to, joked with, left alone. The first time we ever ate there, we had to wait quite a long time for our first course. As it happened we didn't mind. We were enjoying the ambience. He and his one waitress, who is also his wife, were rushed off their feet while his brother was working feverishly in the kitchen. Esteban, however, realised that we had been waiting for about 20 minutes. He came by, explained that he was sorry for the delay which was due to the absence of a staff member that evening. He then asked us if we would accept a bottle of wine on the house. The meal was excellent and we were enjoying watching him work. When it came to the time to pay the bill he brought over two brandies with his compliments and said he hoped we would come again and next time the service would be better!

There have been many next times. The service is always excellent and we usually get a complimentary brandy or equivalent, occasionally an hors d'oeuvre, or an aperitif. We go there a lot!

Retail Store

On a cold Saturday morning in Calgary, Canada, we went into the Hudson's Bay Company department store in the city centre. We were the first people into the store and we needed to buy some sports shirts. In this unfamiliar, huge store we obviously must have looked lost as we gazed around. A maintenance man was passing by, screwdriver in hand. 'Can I help you?' he said. We explained we were looking for some sports clothing. 'Well, on this floor there is a special Olympic display. You might find something there. If not go to the basement and at the foot of the elevator, to your right, is the sporting goods department.' He then took us and showed us the Olympic display and pointed out the elevator to us.

We don't often get this amount of help from store assistants whose job it is. We were impressed by the complete absence of a typical service killer statement: 'I don't know, it's not my job.'

We did buy our shirts and some other products, and the retail staff were skilled service providers too. The products were also good. We went there again the following week to shop.

Taxi Service

We were amazed to discover when getting into a taxi in Copenhagen that we were offered a free daily newspaper. The fact that it was in Danish and we couldn't read it did not lessen the impact. By accident we had hailed a taxi with a sign on it (which we couldn't understand) indicating it was one of a group that gave each passenger a daily newspaper – a simple touch costing pence and probably more than paid for by tips and extra customers.

Garage Service

'I took my car into Lex Brooklands, a Volvo dealer in Leeds. It needed a standard service. When the car was collected it had also been washed outside and cleaned inside. The psychological impact was enormous, far beyond the £2 or so it will have cost.'

When you take your car for a service, typically, you pay a large sum of money and can notice little difference in return.

Health Service

Someone we know was asked to rush to Derby City Hospital where her husband was having difficulties during an operation; his heart had stopped and the situation was serious. She had a neurological complaint which meant that she had a slight tremor in her hands at the best of times, and at this time it was, understandably, much worse. A nurse, knowing the situation but not knowing of her tremor, offered her a cup of tea. She thanked her but explained that in her present condition she would never be able to hold it. A few minutes later the nurse appeared with tea in a feeding cup and offered it to her if she

| A little more goes a long way! |

would not be embarrassed by using it in the waiting room. She was delighted and recounted the incident long after her husband's recovery.

These are all examples of 'that little bit more' at a moment of truth, that ensures that the customer smiles at you instead of you simply smiling at the customer.

SERVICE POINTERS

'I was really impressed recently when I bought a new music centre and went to put the plug on. You know how fiddly it can be to have to strip the ends of the wire, and then you need the earth wire just that bit longer than the live and the neutral. Well, the wires were already stripped and *cut to the right lengths!* It seemed as though somebody had worked out what would irritate the customer most and thought it out. I was so pleased I've been telling everybody about it and that I bought it from the Hi-Fi Centre in Leeds.'

● **Are you always looking for ways of improving the product?**

'The man went to the travel agency to find a particular holiday brochure. There was one assistant who was involved in what sounded like a personal call as he entered the shop. He browsed round the shop but could not find what he wanted. He was in a hurry so he apologetically interrupted the assistant and his call, which was still continuing, to ask whether the brochure was in stock. The assistant broke off his conversation to say, 'If it's not there we haven't got it. Our Head Office never gets its supplies to us right, it gets you down sometimes. If you haven't managed to find one we are probably out of stock. Sorry!' He returned to his call.'

● **What are the lessons here?**

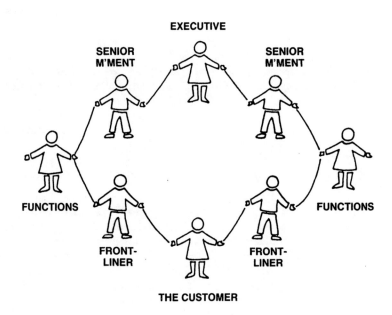

EXECUTIVE

SENIOR
M'MENT

SENIOR
M'MENT

FUNCTIONS

FUNCTIONS

FRONT-
LINER

FRONT-
LINER

THE CUSTOMER

THE SERVICE NETWORK

STEP 5

GIVE GOOD SERVICE TO ONE ANOTHER

If you are not serving a customer, you will be serving somebody who is!

'Sure, I believe in giving good service to the customer, but I also believe in getting it – from our managers and supervisors – and we are definitely not.'

An organisation has to be ready for service management and understand its potential. Inviting staff to be preoccupied with giving the customer a positive experience carries a risk. What is good for the customer is good also for the staff. Staff who do not receive good attention themselves are likely to be somewhat cynical about having to offer it to others.

If staff in an organisation can claim:

- 'We don't support each other around here'
- 'People don't seem to count in this company'
- 'My manager shows no interest in what I do'
- 'Things around here are very unclear'
- 'I'm not sure that my boss knows what I'm good at'
- 'There doesn't seem to be a lot of point in doing more than the minimum'
- 'The best advice in this company is to keep your head down and your mouth shut'
- 'What we are best at is buck-passing'

the organisation needs quickly to examine its vision, whether it is being communicated, whether managers act as role models to staff in providing quality service, and whether the systems are conducive to people giving good service to one another. Whether, in short, there is recognition that the quality of service that reaches the external customer begins with the quality of service that people and functions inside the company give each other.

If in its personnel policies, reward-systems or management style a company conveys a disregard for its staff; if people feel badly done-to, then service training is likely to fall on stony ground.

In any business every job is a service job. There may be staff who say that since they never meet a customer they do not have a service job. 'I'm only an accountant . . . I'm only a secretary . . . I'm only a VDU operator.' Such statements fail to recognise the essential elements in the service network. If the accountants stopped work for a week and nobody was paid, then watch morale and service fall away. If a secretary fails to deal with essential mail or arrange key meetings, watch the manager's effectiveness plummet, and service standards suffer. Watch customer contact staff who are crudely managed, or who do not receive the technical backup they need, and you will see reduced service standards.

The service standards any business wishes to impart to its customers need to be modelled in the service network.

What is good for the customer is good for everybody.

Everybody in a service business needs to recognise who their customer is. Most people's customers will be internal, but their needs and expectations are as relevant as those of external customers.

These points must be built into the service skills training programme, and senior managers must set the tone from the top.

Line managers are also key players in creating and leading a quality service culture. Many of the early approaches to 'putting the customer first' involved high-impact motivation events aimed directly at front-liners. These produced masses of enthusiasm for managing the 'moments of truth', but the results were short-lived. As one CEO of a European airline put it:

'After our quality service programme, we finished up like a poorly reheated frozen meal. All round the edges we were warmed up, but at the centre we had a frozen lump, called line management. We had not recognised its key role and it took us years to recover.'

One theory suggests that 85% of what happens in a business comes down to management, so any initiative which fails to recognise its vital importance is likely to sink without trace. Line managers and supervisors must be trained in the skills of leading and sustaining the service revolution.

Typically, promotion to supervisor and manager has been given to those who were more technically skilled than their peers. Often too late, many realised that technical skills do not equip one for people management. The ability to lead and motivate people is an essential skill for managing in a service business. Here are some other competencies an effective manager is likely to have:

- People skills: the ability to listen, show understanding, be courteous, give time, encourage, support and give recognition to the people they manage.

- Passion: the ability to enthuse, excite, and present a vision that will motivate.

- Leadership qualities: a real belief in people's ability to transcend, which translates into delegation and empowerment. Leadership means achieving through people, offering clear goals, encouraging participation, involvement and creativity. It means setting standards, measuring progress, making success visible. It means making feedback constructive and requiring learning from mistakes. It means making clear 'what' is to be achieved, but leaving the 'how' to your people, trusting them, making them responsible.

Professor Charles Handy suggests that the word 'manager' now has a limited life. It too often means maintaining the status quo, controlling and containing. Now organisations require leaders rather than managers. They want people who release energy and creativity and channel it towards the vision. They want people of a 'can-do' rather than a 'can't-do-it-will-never-work' mentality.

It is significant that many organisations we work with are stripping out layers of management to produce flatter, faster-acting, more flexible organisations, who are more responsive to the customer and the provision of quality. Federal Express, winner of the 1990 Malcolm Baldridge award for Quality and Service in the USA, employs some 90,000 people, but has only 3 levels of management. It is a most impressive operation!

Federal Express has three corporate goals: Service Quality, People and Profit. Its goal of 100% Service Quality is monitored daily when every part of its operation receives a Service Quality Indicator score based on its overnight performance. This score indicates how successful has been the pursuit of a satisfied customer at the end of every transaction. Federal Express has an equally passionate commitment to its second goal, People. Visiting its HQ in Memphis USA, one gets an almost tangible impression of how highly the company values its staff, and how much those staff have pride in themselves and the company as a result. Every six months, all staff in Federal Express are surveyed about their view of management performance. The basic questions amount to 'How easy does your manager make it for you to do a quality job?' and ditto for your manager's manager. At a senior level, some 40% of a manager's pay can be based on a bonus for achievements against corporate goals, one measure of which is continuous improvement in the eyes of the staff. No wonder teamwork is so visible and quality so tangible in the Federal Express culture!

Creating a service climate

What does it feel like to walk into a garage reception area and see staff bang things down on the desk in front of one another? Or visit a restaurant where the waiters are clearly at odds with one another, and all at odds with the chef! Or, as was told to one of us travelling on a North American airline and requesting information on a new frequent flyer programme, 'You don't expect us to know about these things? Another scheme from head office that no one bothers to tell us about!'

Creating a good service climate does not only make day-to-day life for staff more pleasant but there is a 'knock-on' effect to the customer.

Time needs to be spent on a training programme giving clear guidelines as to how the practice of certain daily habits can produce climate changes out of all proportion to the effort involved.

Human beings pass on the kind of treatment they get.

After a bad day at work we are more likely to come home and 'kick the cat'. On the other hand a good day at work can bring blessings for those we come home to. This concept is central to the service treatment the customer receives. Staff treated positively are much more likely to give positive service.

Transactional Analysis, a method of looking at human behaviour developed by Eric Berne, sheds further light on what happens between people when it teaches us about *strokes*.

A stroke is an act of recognition, some form of attention, that one person gives to another. If a person receives no strokes, gets no attention, is ignored by other people, it can be traumatic. One of the most severe forms of punishment is solitary confinement. It strikes at our very nature because essentially we are social beings. We need strokes, recognition and attention, and a complete lack can cause *stroke-hunger*. If we are ignored and feel a nobody, it becomes intolerable. Those unfortunate people who get little or no recognition will make themselves a nuisance rather than be ignored. The evidence is that we prefer negative strokes (critical attention) to no recognition at all.

Negative recognition may be better than no recognition at all, but what is more vital for our well-being is positive recognition. We

The quality of service that reaches the customer begins with the quality of service that staff give each other.

receive a positive stroke when somebody praises our skills or achievements, or acknowledges our qualities.

These strokes must of course be genuine. Insincere compliments are detectable and do harm rather than good. Positive strokes, if they are genuine, are of double value. If our strengths are recognised they become reinforced.

• Tell me you appreciate the support I give you and I am likely to give you even more.

• Tell me that the reports I write are remarkable for their clarity and conciseness, and I am likely to write with even more clarity and conciseness.

In addition, if we are treated positively ourselves we are much more likely to treat others positively. This is a key piece of awareness for service teams.

Service providers *must* model the treatment they want for the customers in their dealings with each other. Service must exist inside an organisation before it can be exported and a positive, encouraging, supportive and confident climate is the basis of it.

A positive work climate is not only built by positive interpersonal contacts. The organisation can assist the process a great deal by designing a positive, creative, exciting environment. The work environment is a shaper of attitudes and behaviour, so investment in it is an investment in service performance. Here are our recommendations on what an organisation can do to create a positive environment:*

• Design events that give a positive start to each month, each year, new projects, new phases. Link these to the vision and goals.

• Make a positive start to days, weeks, meetings; it may only be a matter of coffee, cakes, kind words and helpful ideas.

• Have a 'welcome to our work' sign to greet visitors. Friendly signs have a positive psychological effect.

• Make the workplace beautiful. Attractive settings 'lift' people, ugliness depresses them. Have light rooms, pleasant colours, comfortable chairs and cheerful pictures, especially in reception areas. First impressions count. Ask individuals and groups to produce lists of '10 ways to enhance our environment' and apply the best of them.

---

* A number of these have been contributed by our colleague Mike Pegg.

- Have plenty of plants and trees around. They have a very positive psychological effect.

- Give people a choice of having occasional pleasant, inspiring music as a background to work.

- Display photographs of personnel and customers; photographs rather than just names help to make people more real to each other.

- Have an excellent receptionist, telephonist, commissionaire to make that first impression. Ensure that they are models for, and not substitutes for, everybody else being welcoming.

- Have special events for staff and customers, theme days, days out, special exhibitions, sports events, social outings, treasure hunts, music or cultural events, wine tasting.

- Display your best products or features in the reception area.

- Ask all personnel to use energy positively; have 'no moans, no gripes' contracts.

- Encourage attractive dress and appearance; dress standards promote self-esteem and convey respect for colleagues and customers.

- Encourage and reward stylish ways of working and promoting your products.

- Go public with your goals and aspirations so that staff and customers are constantly aware of the vision.

- Ban the phrase 'Yes . . . but', which introduces so many negative responses. Recognise and reinforce 'Yes . . . and' responses. Challenge people to adapt and build on ideas rather than reject them.

- Make every job as interesting as it can be and ask its owner regularly how it can be made more interesting. Always ensure people have challenge and achievement in their jobs.

- Reward people well.

- Produce posters of what you would like to hear your customers saying about your business; invite everybody to take the steps which would prompt those comments.

- Offer free samples of your products or services so that people can get the taste of them.

- Remember special details about staff and customers, their birthdays, children's names, their favourite colours, foods, music, their hobbies, special talents and skills; and find occasions to show these are remembered.

- Ask everybody to perform one five-minute act of very special service for somebody else each day.

- Celebrate birthdays, anniversaries, spring, summer, autumn, winter, the start of public holidays, return from public holidays, new ideas, new contracts, customer compliments, and anything else which recognises people and their successes.

- Ask everybody to get the first four minutes and the last two minutes right in everyday contacts with colleagues and customers.

- Take good care of everybody and special care of the people who are carrying the heaviest load at particular times.

- Seek out all complaints, internal and external, seek fast effective solutions, and provide that little bit more.

- Provide treats when they are least expected. Chocolates, cakes, a glass of wine, a cup of special coffee, a long lunch break, a bunch of flowers, thank you cards, and any other means of recognising all that people contribute.

- Share out the more boring, mundane work and the opportunities to do what is interesting and creative. Get others involved when anyone has a specially demanding task.

- Produce a 'Ten ways to . . .' book for your business. Ask people to produce ten suggestions for:

  Making the workplace attractive
  Making customers welcome
  Celebrating success
  Improving support for each other
  Having more fun
  Offering better service than your main competitor

  or anything else that would make your business special. Produce a copy of the ideas for everybody and update or expand it every six months by having a half day 'creative party'. Give different people or groups the responsibility for making the ideas happen.

- Spend quality time with each other and take interest in what is happening outside work.

- Recruit positive, confident, energetic staff and support and encourage them at every opportunity. Use your best people to train new recruits.

- Send 'stroke-notes' to staff who do well. A number of notepads with pre-printed headings such as 'Thank God You Did It', are now available. Add your own message to it.

> *When you dance with your customer, who takes the lead?*

- Set up special meetings with your customers. Give them a nice time and ask them:
  'What do we do well?'
  'What could we do better?'

  Listen, learn and do it!

- Create excitement and stimulate interest in a host of ways. Tap into the positive, creative spirit in people, so that they want to join in and other people are attracted to it.

It is vitally important that everybody in the organisation understands the 'Service Network' inside the organisation, and their part in it. Everybody has a customer and everybody is a customer. There must be as much readiness to offer quality and service to 'customers' inside the organisation as there is to external customers. In progressive service companies there will be standards and service contracts agreed between functions and departments inside the business, as a basis for producing the quality required externally.

Volvo Concessionnaires see one of their primary objectives as offering good service to their 280 dealers in the UK. Their regional support teams help dealers to develop their business, offer training to dealer staff in technical and management skills – such as performance appraisals, conflict resolution, interpersonal skills, and customer service. Their 'Do it Right' campaign offered four video based modules as the core of four training sessions which were held in each Dealership over an eight week period. Managers were invited to an Open Learning Seminar to learn how to use the kit with their own staff. 10,000 staff in all went through the programme. Response was immediate and positive. Overnight it changed telephone response. Simultaneously, team training was also offered to all Volvo's own and their dealers' staff.

Some 3,000 staff went through a training programme at Volvo's Daventry training centre called 'Shaping The Future', which launched a new initiative which devolved all warranty issues and decisions on to the dealers, giving them much more responsibility and the opportunity to respond directly to customer's problems instead of having to check out with head office. This, in turn, freed up 75% of Volvo's central customer services teams. Their two new products, Lifetime Care and Careline, were then introduced following massive training programmes.

Training and more training is one of the best ways for an organisation to give good service to its staff.

**Take care of your staff
and they will take care of
the customers!**

SERVICE POINTERS

'My wife had been away on a business trip and was travelling back from Glasgow to Leeds. Unfortunately this was the night of the big north-west gales which created havoc on the roads, cutting off electricity supplies etc. She was due in to Leeds at 8.15pm. Knowing of the weather conditions I wasn't surprised when she was late, but by 10.30pm I was beginning to worry. I called British Rail in Leeds. They were clearly inundated with worried phone calls, but the man I spoke to said, "I'm afraid we have no information about that train. It set off from Glasgow but that's all we know. However, I will contact the various towns it could be at and find out the position for you. Give me your telephone number and I'll ring you back."

'I gave him my number but just assumed that within twenty minutes or so *I* would be doing the ringing back. Ten minutes later I received his call. "We know that your wife's train left Carlisle, but we've drawn a blank after that. All the electrification is down. The problem now is that the later it gets the more difficult it becomes to get information as the stations, especially the smaller ones, are closing down for the night. I know it must be worrying for you. I'll ring you back if I find out any more."

'This he did, ten minutes later, telling me where the train was, how they were sending out a small relief train from Leeds to pick up the passengers. "You should get your wife home by around 2.00am sir, so you'd better have a stiff drink waiting for her!"

'I told this story to many people over the next few weeks. That one assistant had upped BR's image enormously in my eyes.'

- **Why aren't front-line staff always so helpful? Are yours?**

A young woman had bought a saver railway ticket (reduced rate) for weekend travel. She knew there were restrictions on some trains so she checked these carefully. On the return journey she again checked with the ticket office and the person on duty at the barrier and was told the ticket was valid for the train she wished to use. However, when the guard on the train came to collect the tickets he said she would need to pay the excess fare as the ticket could not be used for that train. She told the guard that she had been told otherwise by two railway personnel previously and she did not feel she ought to pay more. The guard mumbled something which implied she was cheating and said he was going off to check his book of regulations. He did not return and the young woman left the train without seeing him again.

- **What will this woman say to her friends about the railway? Do all your staff 'tell the same story'?**

STEP 6

CREATE THE CUSTOMER'S EXPERIENCE

Good service is not just smiling at your customer but getting your customer to smile at you

Are you aware when you walk into a bank, a store, go to a hospital, buy a product, catch a bus, telephone your gas company, etc., that your experience is being managed? No! Good – because the best customer service should not make you feel as if you are being managed.

On the other hand, how often have you experienced the opposite when you are doing one of the above? Not that you are being managed, but that no one cares a hoot what your experience is, or what images you take away.

As businesses grow, it is easy for them to lose sight of the basics. They can become distracted by a great many of the complexities of building the organisation and managing large numbers of staff. If this happens, they lose sight of the simple, essential purpose of any business, which is to satisfy and retain the customer. Quality service companies have staff who keep their eye on that ball, who realise that all else is secondary. They see their job as not simply to sell a product or service, but rather to delight or impress their customer as they do so. Staff working like this understand that at every 'moment of truth' there are three possible outcomes:

- the customer will get less than s/he expects and be disappointed or angry (i.e. the service is memorable because it's awful!)

- the customer will get exactly what s/he expects and therefore it is no big deal (i.e. forgettable because it's neutral!)

- the customer gets service of a higher quality than s/he expects and is delighted (i.e. memorable because it's magic!)

People cannot read your intentions, only your behaviour.

The task is to understand how to create your customer's experience and make it magic!

Successful organisations consciously examine all their moments of truth and plan to utilise them to their and your advantage.

The customer's experience is created by the '4Ps':

Excellent people skills

Superb product

Impressive presentation

Customer-driven processes

THE FIRST 'P' – PEOPLE SKILLS

Tom Peters, speaking to the Directors and top management of an international hotel and leisure group we were working with, congratulated them on the millions of pounds they had invested in redeveloping and upgrading the quality of their properties. His congratulations were qualified, however, by a question to them about how much they were investing in the development of the people who would run those hotels, restaurants and leisure venues. The point he made was that investment in the estate was only buying an entry ticket to the contest. Without those properties they could not compete, but winning the game would depend on the people who staffed them. Customers would be turned on or off by the people, so there was a need to invest in their people skills.

Tom Peters has some straight-talking advice to companies about developing their people: 'If your company is doing well you should double your training budget, if it is doing badly you should quadruple it!' At the end of the day, the skills and attitudes of your people will be what make or break your business.

On our service skills training programmes we identify six major people skills that need to be developed:

Making people feel special

Managing the first 4 and last 2 minutes

Demonstrating a positive attitude

Communicating clear messages

Showing high energy

Working well under pressure

To help people remember these six skills we can use the following mnemonic.

The customer comes 1st where **comes 1st** stands for

C   = clear messages
O   = OK attitude
M   = making people feel special
E   = energy
S   = service under pressure

1st = 4 minutes and last 2 minutes

Making people feel special

The basis for all quality contact is a real respect for the person, which is also the basis of service, but this has to be demonstrated in behaviour. For example, we feel special when people:

• listen to us and respond to what we say;

• go to some trouble to provide what we need;

• give us time and quality attention;

• use our name when appropriate;

• are courteous, polite and welcoming;

• show interest in our ideas and experiences and ask questions to find out more;

• seek our comfort and solutions to our difficulties;

• provide that little bit more than we expect.

Part of making people feel special is to recognise their *uniqueness*. Each of us is a mixture of genes, personality and experience which makes us a one-off. What excites one person may bore another. What one regards as valuable will be unimportant to another. We can make generalisations about what people have in common, but we must not lose sight of the fact that each of us is different.

British Airways' clients registered this quite clearly when they said in a service survey:

**'Treat us as people, as individuals,
don't just process us!'**

Your customers will get better when you do.	

At the moments of truth, we need to recognise that the customer's world and experience is different from our own. At this point what customers want from us is to *understand* them, to put ourselves in their place, to see their point of view. The best service providers show understanding. They look at any situation through the eyes of the customer. We are likely to feel understood when:

- people pick up not just what we say but also how we feel;
- they show in their faces that they are on our wavelength, concerned if we are, amused if we are, and respond accordingly;
- they don't allow their views to deny our experience, but accept what we say;
- they adjust their views on the basis of what we say.

In quality service situations the customers always feel understood, always feel that the provider is seeing things from their point of view.

A third key area of people skills is the ability to inspire trust. In situations of quality service the customer does *not* feel manipulated or controlled but *does* experience the provider as genuine, trustworthy and reliable. Trust does not just materialise, it has to be built and maintained, it is a keystone of excellent service.

People show they are genuine and can be trusted when:

- they are open and honest about themselves;
- they take responsibility;
- they admit mistakes and shortcomings when they exist;
- they keep promises;
- they follow through and show they are reliable;
- they are consistent;
- they put themselves out to help others;
- what you see is what you get!

Excellent service always conveys and promotes trust by conveying the genuineness of the provider.

When what is communicated at moments of truth is that:

the customer is **respected**
and **understood**
and treated **genuinely**

the foundations are laid for quality service.

First 4 and last 2 minutes

We *can* make a difference to our customers' experience by using service skills. The biggest threat however is a lack of time. When rushed or under pressure, our best intentions are most at risk. The temptation may be to rush all we have to do because there is more waiting to be done. Dealing with customers at such a time needs a steady hand because lasting impressions are built from first impressions.

The *first 4 minutes* of any meeting are the most important. In that brief span a great many impressions are made and conclusions drawn. People rapidly assess how important they are, or are not, in the eyes of the other person, how much the other cares, is interested, concerned, enthusiastic, willing to help or otherwise.

It seems we give each other the first 4 minutes as an opportunity, after that we make up our mind about people. If we are dealing with a customer in that time and are officious, impatient, impersonal or inattentive then a great deal is lost. If we are pleasant, courteous and responsive we have established a solid foundation.

Rapport not built in the first 4 minutes is difficult to establish later.

This is true also when it comes to how we manage the first 4 minutes with our colleagues and those we live with, every meeting of every day. Good or bad starts can be made:

- at breakfast
- on arrival at work
- at meetings
- on telephones
- on returning home

Sensitive, genuine, positive attention given at those moments of truth can make a huge difference to the way things go from that point. For example, how did you spend your first 4 minutes with the first person you encountered this morning? Was that a good start?

How did you spend your first 4 minutes with the first person you met at work this morning?

But it is not just first impressions that are crucial.

In Shakespeare's version of *Antony and Cleopatra* it is interesting to note that however violent the rows between the two of them, once Cleopatra had accepted that Antony really was leaving, her attitude changed dramatically. She was loving, understanding, coquettish because she knew that

the last impression lingers longest.

In the first 4 minutes you are your organisation.

We need to put as much thought into what we do when customers leave us as we do when they make contact.

And how do we maximise the first 4 and last 2 minutes?

- Avoid ritual or routine activity or standard phrases.
- Smile. Even smile when you answer the telephone – it sounds! And don't let a telephone ring more than three times.
- Avoid moans, groans and negative comments, about self, weather, work, another person, etc.
- Deal with customers in turn, make every customer your favourite.
- Avoid rushing or doing too many things at once.
- Get the customer's name as soon as possible and use it.
- Look at people. Take an interest in them. Pay attention to how they are, what they are doing and saying.
- Don't chat to other staff when customers are about.
- Greet them with some enthusiasm and look for positive, genuine things to say about them.
- Assess what kind of help they want: to be left alone, to be approached, to be chatted to, to be direct with.
- Have something positive to say when you or they leave.
- Get a definite closure, don't let it just ebb away.

**When you're serving a customer you're
on stage: are you dressed for the part?
do you know your lines?
do you understand the play?**

An OK attitude

Demonstrating a positive attitude is crucial. The service givers' attitudes to themselves and to their clients are the service launch-pad. Our attitudes shape our responses.

The Transactional Analysis model of human behaviour provides us with a shorthand way of understanding what happens between people. In terms of a view of ourselves we can be anywhere on the continuum:

'*If you're all
wrapped up in
yourself, you are
overdressed.*'
Kay Halverson
and Karen Hess

I'M OK -- I'M NOT OK

A person with an 'I'm OK' attitude sees herself positively. She will be aware of her skills and qualities, and her value as an individual, and have basic confidence in herself. People operating from this position have no illusions about perfection. They are aware of shortcomings and potential in themselves, but see those as areas to work on rather than reasons to doubt oneself.

Somebody whose basic attitude is 'I'm not OK' lives with self-doubt and self-criticism. His experience is consistently negative, focusing on faults and failings, seeing little value in himself and seeing all contributions he might make to situations as largely futile.

As well as attitudes to ourselves we subconsciously carry round attitudes relating to other people. They also can be seen on a continuum:

YOU'RE OK --------------------------------- YOU'RE NOT OK

A person whose basic attitude to others is 'You're OK' sees other people as worthwhile, significant and of value. She will see their talents and their qualities, she will be aware of their skills and contributions in any transaction.

On the other hand, some people do see others as basically 'Not OK'. This attitude causes us to view people as not worthwhile. We will be aware of them as nuisances, as problems, as irritants. We will see their inadequacies and failings before we see anything else.

We can piece together these attitudes towards ourselves and others and see how they can explain a great deal of what happens between people. The continua combine to give us four quadrants (Diagram 4):

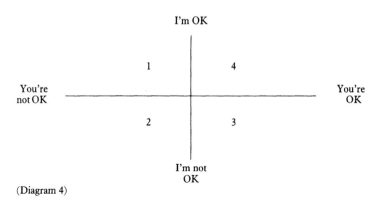

(Diagram 4)

Quadrant 1
I'M OK. YOU'RE NOT OK
A person operating from this quadrant might be seen as arrogant, domineering, prejudiced, devaluing, opinionated, patronising, rigid, impersonal, not able to listen, bureaucratic, judgmental, critical, treating people as nuisances, irritants or stupid. People in this quadrant are often impatient, frequently negative, and can be aggressive.

Quadrant 2
YOU'RE NOT OK. I'M NOT OK
Somebody coming from this position could be seen as low in energy, very negative, unlikely to care or take much trouble, apathetic, contributing very little, lacking commitment, unresponsive, lacking initiative and quick to accept defeat.

Quadrant 3
YOU'RE OK. I'M NOT OK
Somebody whose standpoint is from this quadrant might lack confidence, feel inadequate, play helpless, be submissive, lack sharpness and be servile and non-assertive.

Quadrant 4
I'M OK. YOU'RE OK
People with this standpoint are most likely to be seen as confident in themselves and others, responsive, action-orientated, calm under pressure, rational, energised, creative, flexible, prepared to see others' points of view, a good listener, interested in others and working to solve problems.

Awareness of our basic attitudes helps greatly in service situations. Quality service always happens in quadrant 4. The provider of service acts positively and confidently, using skills and talents for the benefit of the customer because the customer is recognised as valuable and worthy of quality attention. In other quadrants there could be patterns of demeaning the customer, or of servility, which are very different from quality service.

The quadrants are sometimes given other labels:

Quadrant 1 = Win/Lose
Quadrant 2 = Lose/Lose
Quadrant 3 = Lose/Win
Quadrant 4 = Win/Win

> You never get a
> later chance to
> make a last
> impression.

Sometimes after a transaction people emerge feeling they have won or lost. In this context, winning can mean feeling that you got the better of somebody or gained some advantage over another person. Losing means you come away feeling you have been put down, taken advantage of, or you have 'lost out' in some way. In quadrants 1, 2 and 3 somebody loses, be it the service provider, the customer or both. In quadrant 4 both parties emerge feeling good about their interaction.

Quality service in fact produces a
WIN/WIN/WIN
result

The idea of the quadrants is not that anybody inhabits any particular quadrant permanently. Depending on our mood, our situation and many other factors we can occupy different quadrants at different times. The value in the idea is:

We do have a choice of quadrants – by being aware, telling ourselves the right things, developing our skills, we can finish in quadrant 4 more often.

We can invite other people to join us in quadrant 4 – our customers as well as ourselves will come from a variety of quadrants. By maintaining quadrant 4 behaviour ourselves, listening, being confident, responsive, being clear and assertive we can model a way of working that others will follow. We can change other people's patterns by being the shining example of how we would like them to be!

Communicating clear messages

In our service training we pay particular attention to the skills of communicating clear messages.

We need to be aware that:

- **People cannot read our minds** – they cannot tell what we are thinking;

 But

- **They pick up messages from our behaviour** – the things we do or fail to do, the things we say, or do not say;

- **We are always communicating** – whether we realise it or not;

- **Up to 90% of what we communicate will not be in words** – non-verbal communication, or body language, is most important;

> *Service is like love . . . it is not the word that matters it's the actions!*

- **We do not always communicate what we intend** – developing our skills will help us to get our behaviour in line with our intentions. Our task at moments of truth, therefore, is to behave towards our customers in such a way that they feel special.

To give good service we need to become more effective at **sending** and **receiving** clear messages.

The skills of **sending** clear messages to your customers involve:

- Knowing *what* you want to say.

- Deciding *when* and *where* is the appropriate time to say it.

- Judging *how* best to say it – assertively, roundabout, etc.

- Keeping it simple.

- Speaking clearly.

- Making eye-contact.

- Monitoring the customer's response for signs of confusion, irritability, acceptance, etc.

- Using appropriate language.

- Making sure *what* you say is consistent with *how* you say it (e.g. not saying you're sorry through gritted teeth).

The skills of **receiving** messages from your customers involve:

- Getting rid of 'baggage': thoughts and feelings that creep in about what has happened before – with the previous customer, with the same customer on another occasion, with a colleague, your boss, or a home problem.

- Active listening, hearing what the customer is really saying.

- Checking out if you're not sure what was being said.

- Listening for the feelings behind the words.

- Getting rid of prejudices and suppositions.

- Remembering that hearing something with which we disagree will mean that it is all too easy to switch off or get angry. When we become judgmental or begin to plan our counterattack we are likely to have stopped listening.

Ian Ferguson, of London Life, says
'I find a useful way of getting this message across on courses here at London Life is to liken communication to the words, the music and the dance, where words = words, music = tone of voice, and dance = body language. I make the point that if you attend a musical and all three components are not synchronised then you can tell there is something wrong. The same happens when we talk to someone: if the words, tone of voice and body language are not giving the same message, it is obvious something is wrong and this we call insincerity.'

After your next contact with a customer, sit down quietly with this list and see how many you achieved.

Showing high energy

Can you remember the last time you walked into an office and saw someone staring into space, reading a magazine, painting her nails? Or someone else reading his morning paper? Or when you walked into a shop and the assistants were sitting down, or leaning on the counter chatting to one another, or looking generally bored?

What impressions do these give? The research on the skills of making relationships shows quite clearly that people are attracted towards people who:

• Make them feel special.

• Have positive attitudes to themselves and others.

• Communicate clearly and non-judgmentally.

• Demonstrate high energy, look as if they are glad to be alive, behave as if they have something to offer, and move as if they have a purpose.

Some people naturally have more high energy than others, and this could have implications for who is given face-to-face contact with your customers. For your front-liners pick staff who have high people skills and high energy. You cannot afford to take risks with your front-liners.

But whatever our potential for energy, it will be affected by how we think about ourselves. People who fit into quadrant 4 and even quadrant 1 of our diagram are likely to have more energy than those

'If you don't
genuinely like
your customers,
the chances are
they won't buy.'
Thomas Watson

in quadrants 2 and 3. So, attitude is closely linked to energy. But how about lifestyle?

Research on lifestyle shows that we will be fitter and consequently closer to our optimum energy levels if we:

- Take regular exercise – which must be aerobic, that is vigourous exercise of at least 20 minutes for three times a week. (But don't just rush into it if you are not used to it! – build up slowly and if in doubt consult your doctor.)

- Don't smoke.

- Maintain our correct body weight

- Get 7–8 hours sleep each night

- Eat a balanced diet

- Drink alcohol moderately (0–2 drinks a day)

- Eat regular meals – and stop to sit down and do so.

Interestingly, all this discussion relates to our next and final people skill:

Working well under pressure

Service awareness and skills make service jobs more satisfying to do. The satisfaction of good service flows backwards and forwards between the giver and receiver. Achieving standards is the first challenge, maintaining them is the next. That requires particular care at times of great pressure.

Life rarely flows steadily; it has its ups and downs. We can expect high service standards when people are at their best, but what about when they are not? Service training needs to provide service givers with the skills to look after themselves, so that they are at their best most of the time.

There are interesting links made between work performance and pressure. Ask people how they feel about pressure, and you are likely to get largely negative reactions. They will equate pressure with stress and link it with words like worry, anxiety, pain, sleeplessness and so on. Under pressure or stress they say we are not at our best and service suffers. But look at the message in Diagram 5.

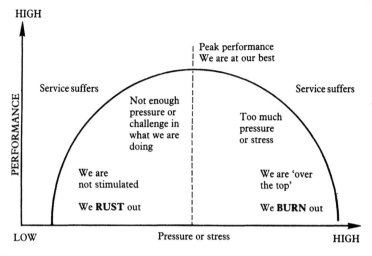

(Diagram 5)

Pressure or stress

Service jobs need to be challenging and stimulating for us to give of our best. Tasks which are too easy, which make no demands on us, which we can do in our sleep, do not bring out our best performance. On the other hand tasks that are too demanding or too numerous push us into the area of too much stress. That not only impairs our service performance, it can also damage our health.

Service skills, therefore, involve being able to look after ourselves so that we are at our optimum as often as possible. This means learning to spot when we are under or over the limit. In general terms the signs are:

Under-stressed
We experience a lack of interest or enthusiasm for what we are doing. We can feel that what we are doing is futile and we will be bored and lacking in energy. At times like this the world seems grey and drab and it is difficult to apply our energy to providing service.

Over-stressed
We feel anxious or confused. We will not think clearly nor solve problems effectively. We will forget things and panic more easily. Our

co-ordination will be impaired, our work will be poorly organised. We lack confidence and respond slowly. Service inevitably will suffer.

Optimum level
We will be alert and self-confident. We will think and respond quickly, be interested and involved in what we have to do, and carry out our tasks in an energetic easy manner. We will feel good, perform well and be enthusiastic. Service excellence comes from people operating at this level.

In service training people can learn to spot the clues as to when they are not at their best. These might include:

- inability to sleep;

- a feeling of constant fatigue;

- lack of appetite;

- a desire to eat when there is a particular problem;

- frequent headaches;

- shortness of breath;

- frequent sighing;

- inability to relax, sit still or concentrate;

- a constant feeling of unease;

- constant irritability with colleagues or family;

- a feeling of boredom or lifelessness;

- inability to have a good laugh;

- inablity to concentrate or finish a job.

If two or more of these clues are in evidence then the person experiencing them needs to give him or herself some special attention.
There are many strategies and methods of coping with being under pressure and off peak.
You can:

Develop a fitness programme. There are many effective and not too time-consuming fitness programmes, which can produce that feeling of well-being. Being on top of the world is conducive to good service.

Eat wholesomely. 'We are what we eat'; junk food or a generally stodgy diet does not promote the sharpness that service situations require.

Learn relaxation or meditation. This ability to take the tension out of our minds and bodies can help us at 'crunch' points.

Learn good time-management. To organise time so that one can accomplish one's task, encourages that important feeling of being in control.

Develop problem-solving and decision-making skills. The ability to see creative solutions to difficulties and take the steps to accomplish them.

Develop a support system – have people to talk to. Service providers can provide a service to each other in offering support and encouragement, especially at times of particular difficulty or pressure.

Learn constructive self-talk. The ability to tell oneself positive, rational messages as a way of life, avoiding the low energy and bad feelings which result from negative self-talk.

You can also adopt some of these simple but valuable tips:

- Take at least 10 minutes per day to walk in the park;

- Work no more than 10 hours per day and 5½ days per week;

- Allow at least 30 minutes for each meal;

- Eat slowly;

- Have 'minibreaks' and one complete away-from-it-all holiday each year;

- Eat a wholesome, balanced diet;

- Have time to yourself, somewhere to be alone;

- Listen to relaxing music;

- Be kind to somebody, support other people;

- Cultivate the garden;

- Keep a pet;

- Have a massage;

- Concentrate on moving, walking and talking more slowly;

- Avoid too many changes at once;

- Define your problem clearly, act early;
- Accept you are not the answer to everything;
- Don't dwell on the past, there is no future in it;
- Don't always strive to win;
- Ask for help when you need it;
- Don't bottle up your feelings, but avoid hostility;
- Have a laugh or giggle regularly;
- Set realistic deadlines, build in success;
- Finish one thing before starting another;
- Give yourself a treat when you have earned it, and sometimes when you have not;
- Don't talk 'shop' when you are supposed to be having a break or relaxing;
- 'Count your blessings', force yourself to remember two good things about the day before you go to sleep;
- Learn to say 'no', it makes your 'yes' even more valuable;
- Be clear what your values and priorities are.

The organisation can do a great deal to help staff manage pressure. It can:

Offer service skills training: this will mean that customers will be less likely to find themselves in situations which are the cause of their becoming difficult, hostile and obnoxious.

Ensure that managers give good service to their staff.

Make sure the product is worth selling: so that the staff can take pride in what they make and sell.

Make sure the physical environment is comfortable and attractive to work in: this gives a clear message to staff that they are considered valuable.

THE SECOND 'P' – PRODUCT

A manager of a branch office of an insurance company had a £15,000 allowance to purchase a new car. He knew the model he wanted and

> *Never, never pay more attention to the people side of service than you do to your product and to how it gets delivered and backed up.*

visited the main dealer garage. After 20 minutes in the showroom, he was so appalled by the off-hand treatment he received from the staff that he left saying, 'They didn't seem to be bothered about doing business with me at all. I liked the car, but I will take my money somewhere where people care!' In this case, product quality was betrayed by a lack of people skills in the operation.

There is a restaurant in London where the people skills are excellent, the customer really is put first, the decor is very attractive, and reluctantly, we don't go there any more. Why? The food rises to the heights of mediocrity.

A friend bought a cord-free iron recently. It looks very attractive, there is excellent after-sales service, the people at the shop are helpful and courteous – but the iron is lousy! Because three out of four aspects of the customer's service experience were good, she might use the shop again, but probably not, because from her point of view the shop sells poor products.

As Tom Peters says:

**Good service is not a
substitute for junk**

There is sometimes a danger that an organisation can become so preoccupied with developing excellent people skills that it can forget to look just as closely at its basic products.

An organisation must commit itself to improving constantly the quality of its products. In Japan this is axiomatic. Their word for it is *kaizen*, which means 'ongoing improvement involving everyone'. This also involves finding out what the customer wants.

Edward Heath, after visiting China, quoted Dong-Xiao Ping to sum up what customer-oriented production is really about:

'The Americans and the Europeans come to us offering splendid goods and enquiring how much we want to buy . . . the Japanese approach is to ask us what we want, how much we can afford to pay and then produce the goods.'

THE THIRD 'P' – PRESENTATION

People do judge books by their covers and quality service business will be alert to this. As customers, we are influenced, for better or worse, by the features that 'surround' the product or service we receive. These features can include:

- the physical environment into which the customer comes: how does this look, sound, smell, feel, and what are the messages it carries about the company's attitude to the customer?

- the appearance of the staff the customer meets;

- the quality of brochures and marketing materials;

- the tonc and lay-out of correspondence;

- the condition and appearance of company transport.

All of these will play a part in creating the customer's experience. Quality service means attending to every detail!

One hotel we visited while working in Hong Kong has a most beautiful, even stunning, foyer. You can watch new customers come in and gaze around in awe at this most imposing setting. It is very impressive and attractive, but in the opinion of the manager its impact lasts for two visits. After that, he says, what the customer notices most is the reception they get from the staff who check them in. Quality service is an intermeshing of many factors.

The Leeds Building Society is exploring all the features of its business as part of its 'Customer First' initiative. It is looking at all activities from the customer's point of view. As a result, it realised that over the years many of its branches had become admin-centres in which two-thirds of the space was given over to paper and staff. In a massive refurbishment programme, those branches are now giving two-thirds of the space to the customer, and offering a stylish, open, welcoming, professional, setting in which to meet. The Leeds, of course, is also working on all the other 'Ps' in its approach to 'Customer First'.

Increasingly, design is becoming a major factor in the conceptualisation of products and services as well as in the more predictable areas of merchandising.

Sir Terence Conran has based an entire retail empire on style. All Habitat products are designed by them, not the manufacturer, so that a clear style can be identified by the customer. He was so appalled at how his original furniture was displayed in stores that this became the incentive for him to open his own store to display it in his own way:

'The strength of the original Habitat design-based formula has been in selling furniture in a colourful ambience partially created by the non-furniture merchandise. We have sold products which all measure up to a good standard of design and appear to have been selected with "one pair of eyes". We have invested in a large design team, to ensure exclusivity, well-designed merchandise and strong graphic style. Moreover, we have never been satisfied with existing standards.'*

In the retail trade the Body Shop, as already discussed, although eschewing wasteful packaging, has put a huge emphasis on attractive but standardised, clearly identifiable design that appeals to sight, smell and touch.

The Next Group has adopted a similar approach. Next shops increasingly look like works of art themselves, with everything colour co-ordinated from clothes to furniture and soft furnishings.

Benetton shows that continental Europe can also see the value of design-led products, packaging and merchandising.

Just ask people who work for any of these chains how they feel about being identified with their shops. Quality creates pride.

When Jan Carlzon took over an ailing SAS, one of his first acts was to spend money the airline could hardly afford on new uniforms and regalia for the staff. Sir Colin Marshall attracted considerable controversy doing exactly the same at British Airways, commissioning a new logo and aircraft design for £1 million and outfitting all staff in new uniforms.

If staff feel good about their products and feel good about the place in which they work, the foundations are there for the rest of the service package.

Walk into your premises as a customer would do for the first time. Describe it.

- What are the messages in that physical setting?

- Is there anything you would want to do to change them?

- And what about your own immediate workspace?

Have a contract with a colleague. Visit one another's workspaces and describe them as a stranger would, entering them for the first time. Does your workspace communicate what you intend it to communicate?

THE FOURTH 'P' – PROCESSES

We knew one financial services company which analysed its service quality against the '4Ps'. It decided its level of people skills was high,

---

* Quoted by Ronnie Lessem in his book *Entrepreneurship* Wildwood House, Aldershot, 1987 and reproduced with permission of Gower Publishing Group.

its products were good and its presentation or packaging was impressive. Unfortunately, its staff were clear that all their efforts were impeded by processes, practices and procedures at Head Office that were less than quality. As some said, 'We seem to have a service black-hole at Head Office; our administration and technology back-up is so poor that quality service at the sharp end is undermined.'

So, in addition to continuous improvement in the other three 'Ps', quality service means making all processes customer-driven; organising so that the customer can get what s/he wants when s/he wants it.

Gert Jensen, a Danish colleague of ours tells with feeling of how he has to turn up at airports one hour before a flight just so that all the staff can dazzle him with their newly developed people skills!

The point he is making is that it *is* possible to be so focused on people skills in service provision that the way the service is organised can get overlooked. He says that the best service an airline could offer a busy consultant like himself would be to require him to check in only 15 minutes before his flight.

Gert will be impressed to know that British Midland now offer a 15 minutes check in at Leeds–Bradford airport for domestic flights, and their return fights from Heathrow require only 20 minutes. Fortunately, their people skills quotient is very high too.

To relieve pressure on their staff, banks introduced 'hole-in-the-wall' banking – electronic cash points. Banks are now discovering that since the 'Big Bang' in the City, they now need increasingly to sell their services. To do that they want more face-to-face contact with their clients. Some of them are beginning service skills training programmes for their staff, who return from their courses enthused and ready to demonstrate their new skills to their customers, and what do they find? Many customers prefer to go to the 'hole-in-the-wall'. They have no desire to go into a bank unless absolutely necessary.

A survey of high street banks carried out by the Grass Roots Group* in early 1988 showed that cashpoint facilities were easily the second most important factor influencing people in their choice of bank.

How customers choose a bank

Factors which most influenced people in their choice of bank:

Close to home/work	51%
Cashpoint facilities	38%
Parental recommendation	24%

* Major Research Study into Customer Handling of Banks and Building Societies.

Friendly staff 22%
Free banking 20%
Saturday opening 13%
Free gift 4%
Advertising 2%
Other recommendation 7%

It is interesting to note that the first two factors are both *process* items. The third one probably does refer to *people skills* and *product* over the years, but the most obvious people factor, friendly staff, is the fourth on the list. Having said that, 22% of customers quote that as a significant factor, more than quoted for a *product* item such as free banking.

British Telecom have made customer-driven practices a priority with CSS (Customer Service Systems), the world's first computer system designed to draw together all the main elements of customer service. Customers dial one number, 150, and get straight through to what BT calls the **Front Office.**

The person answering the call should be able to deal with virtually any sales order, accounts problem, fault report or any general enquiry on the spot. This is due to a massive investment in information technology. As soon as a call is taken the staff can pull up on screen a thumbnail sketch of the customer's individual record. It gives the basics: name, address, the number and type of installation and any faults recorded in the past six months. The customer will be addressed by name almost immediately, and a customer contact registry completes the picture. This displays on screen the customer's last five transactions with BT.

So, what is quality service?

A great deal of service quality is people-based. People's treatment of the client, and of each other at the same time, is a key element, but it is not the whole story. The service microscope has to be focused on every dimension of the business. The way the product or service is delivered has to be customer-driven:

- It is not good enough to give the customer good attention if the telephone system you use has poor reception and means a long holding time.

- It is frustrating for customer contact staff to get everything right with the customers face to face, only to find they can't get the data they need quickly, because they don't have appropriate computer back up.

'There's no such thing as a commodity.'
Theodore Levitt

- It takes the edge off quality contact with the customer when paperwork goes out looking less than stylish because the office copying system is primitive.

Creating the right internal service climate will contribute to improving processes. This might mean implementing cross-functional teams, or applying what you learn from customer research, or asking staff which processes or practices are impeding quality service to the customer.

Accounts departments can sometimes undo what the rest of the company has built up because of incomprehensible bills, double invoicing, officious demands. This is not to deny that it is vital to collect bad debts, but how often do accounts departments think of creative or even humorous ways of collecting money, prior to using the dagger or sledge-hammer?

We liked the following final demand:

'If you fail to pay this bill within 30 days we are turning your account over to a human.'

SERVICE POINTERS

The businessman checked in at the hotel he had used twice before in the last 12 months. He was made very welcome at reception and shown to his room which was beautifully clean and well lit. He had had a very hard day and was looking forward to his first drink. There was a knock at the door: room service with his favourite drink, Campari and fresh orange juice with lots of ice.

'A drink sir, to say welcome to our hotel. It's good to see you back here. Please don't hesitate to let us know if there is anything you need. This drink comes with the compliments of the manager, Mr Moxon.'

- **We all like to feel special. What do you do to help your customers feel special?**

One of our consultants was meeting with a potential client at a hotel in Birmingham on a Friday lunchtime. The client was the managing director and owner of his company. They had an excellent lunch, retired to the lounge for coffee and their discussions went well on into the afternoon. At one point the client announced that his company owned some racehorses and one of them was running in the 3.30 race that afternoon and it was on TV. Because it was an expensive hotel, all

> *There is no such thing as an insignificant improvement.*
> Tom Peters

the rooms had a TV but there were none in the public areas. The client went to the receptionist and asked if it was possible to watch this race on a TV anywhere in the hotel. She looked nonplussed and said that unfortunately there wasn't one available.

The consultant then pointed out that every room had a TV, and that being Friday afternoon there must be a number of available rooms. The receptionist had to check out with someone else to see if this was possible. It was and they went to watch the race – which the client's horse lost!

When paying the bill for lunch, the client was also asked for £10 for 'hire of room'. He paid it, but afterwards it was the charge that was talked about not the service! He has never returned to that hotel!

* **This is an excellent example of a lost service opportunity. How could it have been handled?**

* **Do your front-line staff have the authority to respond directly to customers' needs without always having to check out up the hierarchy?**

> 'Excellent service is not about being
> 1000% better at one thing but 1% better
> at a thousand things.'
>
> Jan Carlzon

STEP 7

PROFIT FROM COMPLAINTS

You don't have to be ill to get better

No one likes to hear complaints – correct? Of course we don't, but we need to learn to treasure them. Complaints can be the lifeblood of your business. Does that sound extreme? Maybe, but what does it mean if you never hear complaints?

- Your service is perfect?

- Your customers are too frightened to complain – they just go away?

- Your customers just cannot be bothered to complain – and they go away too?

- Your customers have tried complaining and nothing changes – so they also leave?

One thing you can be sure of is that your service will never be perfect. People will always be too individual for your service package to appeal to everyone in your target group at all times.

Your aim should be to reduce a torrent of complaints to a trickle, but if that trickle dries up you should begin to ask yourself why, rather than sit around congratulating yourself.

Complaints can be the
educators of your business.
Your biggest problem will be unearthing
them

Take a look at what was discovered about complaints by the TARP (Technical Assistance Research Programmes, Washington DC)

organisation who investigated customer behaviour in over 200 companies in the USA and Canada.
They found:

- Most dissatisfied customers do not complain. The average business does not hear from 96% of its unhappy customers.

- For every complaint received there will be another 26 customers with problems, at least 6 of these will be serious.

- Complaints are not made because people think it's not worth the time and effort, they don't know how or where to complain, or they believe the company would be indifferent to them.

- Non-complainers are the least likely group to buy from the company again. A complainer who gets a response is more likely to come back. Between 65% and 90% of non-complainers will never buy from you again and you will never know why.

- A company needs to welcome complaints as a second chance to keep a customer.

- Even a complaint made but not satisfactorily dealt with makes the customer 10% more likely to come back – just being able to complain helps.

- When customers complain and the matter is dealt with satisfactorily 54% will buy again. If the complaint is dealt with quickly and efficiently the retention rate rises to 90–95%. (The above figures refer to major purchases such as domestic appliances, a motor car or an insurance policy).

- For smaller purchases such as food items, clothes or household goods 37% of unhappy non-complainers will not purchase again, 82% of complainers will if their complaint is handled well.

- Damage may not be restricted to the person with a complaint. A customer who has had an unpleasant experience will tell an average of 9–10 other people. 13% of those with a complaint will tell more than 20 others.

- When a complainer has received a satisfactory response they will tell only half the number of other people and will talk about it positively.

Avis Europe, and particularly its Director of Customer Satisfaction Linda Lash, have used TARP research to prove to its managers the value of learning from customers, and recovering, if ever service quality is not 100%. Currently Avis is the leading car rental company in Europe and has grown its pre-tax profits from £26 million to £72 million in the last 4 years. At Avis they believe:

Customer satisfaction performance is reported on at every Board meeting alongside financial performance. The 'Avis Customer Satisfaction Tracking System' measures customer opinion of Avis service and willingness to buy again. This information builds into a Market Damage Simulation Model which attaches figures to this formula:

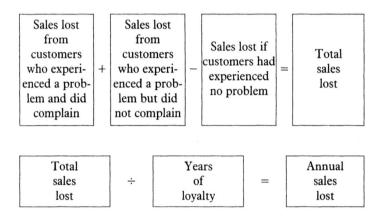

The results of such analysis establish the value of tracking down every unhappy customer, finding out what were the causes of the problem and what it would take to put things right. The only acceptable result is a satisfied customer who will use Avis again. This is the kind of awareness and dedication that proves again and again the Avis claim, 'We try harder!'

How to unearth complaints

Researching your customers in an ongoing way is one way of ensuring that you identify needs, but it also begins to unearth irritants and, best of all, potential irritants before they develop into fully-fledged problems.

We have seen many different attempts to do this, some systematic, some non-systematic, some boring, some fun. It can be difficult to get the right balance.

Systematic methods

- Customer survey: these might be random or using a quota sampling technique.

  Volvo send out questionnaires to all their customers after they have bought a car and then again after one and two years. They manage to get a 40–50% response rate. There are also open-ended questions and the answers to these are all read and responded to. From this Volvo establish their Customer Satisfaction Index and each dealership can be assessed against this.

- Telephone surveys are becoming increasingly popular. Kwik-Fit customer service department telephone at random 100 customers per month to check on customer satisfaction.

- Staff surveys: tapping in to all the customer intelligence that staff possess – especially your front-liners.

- Setting up a system so that all complaints are written up and centralised, with one person having the responsibility for monitoring them all and reporting back.

- Monitoring your own staff performance; this is a technique that should only be used after careful consideration and with the backing of the staff.

Seatons, the Ford dealers at Yeovil, use an agency which, every two months, telephones all departments, posing as customers. Conversations are taped and later played to the employee. Trevor Curphey, a member of Ford's retail strategy team says, 'They do feel that they've got Big Brother looking over their shoulder. But the customer is King and when they listen to themselves they often realise that attitudes are lacking.' He quickly points out that in return there are employee car lease and very low finance schemes and company pensions.*

Selfridges uses a 'mystery shopper' who systematically visits each department over a period of time and rates it on a number of criteria. Using a similar technique, Gateway Hosts were able to monitor the effectiveness of the customer care training programme for all their

---

* Quoted in *The Financial Times*, 11 May, 1988.

staff, and to demonstrate clearly the value of the training. TWA have a team of Quality Assessors who, incognito, travel the globe in all classes of service and appraise the minutest details of passenger care.

Non-systematic methods

These usually rely on the customer taking the initiative to respond to an invitation to give feedback. We know from the TARP findings just how difficult it can be to get customers to do this and the techniques, therefore, often need to be a little gimmicky to attract customers to give up their time to talk back to you. The problem with this is that gimmicky techniques are most likely to attract people who like gimmicks!

Some of the techniques we have seen used in this way certainly do provide customer data; the problem comes in not knowing how representative it is. Some of the techniques we describe below have become talking points and as such help to build a positive image for the business. But techniques like these, although not systematic, can sometimes be the germs of new service ideas.

Video-points

British Airways introduced Video-points into Terminals 1 and 4 at Heathrow. These are booths, a little like those that you sit inside to take your own passport photograph. Once you are inside you are invited to make your own video of yourself talking to BA about how you have found their service.

Some customers who have used this comment that you do feel you have a direct line to the CEO.

Customer hot-lines

Some US research suggests that this is one of the most effective methods. In the US Polaroid discovered from analysing its toll-free telephone calls that including batteries in their film packs would eliminate one of the most frequent customer complaints. The General Electric Answer Centre offers a 24-hour-a-day service provided by 140 telephone staff backed up by 50 technical specialists. It handles over 2 million calls a year, of which only a small fraction are complaints.

A useful practice is to organise periodical meetings of the telephone answering staff to discuss their sense of what is happening in the market-place.

John Scully, president of Apple Computers, believed so strongly in the value of this method, that he personally answered a number of hot-line calls to get an uncensored sampling of customer attitudes. In addition, of course, this models from the top the message that it is crucial to listen to customers.

Tom Farmer, chairman of Kwik-Fit, likewise, commits one evening a fortnight to personally ringing customers to enquire about how they had found the service the previous day.

Feedback cards

Many hotels now place little feedback cards in their rooms for you to fill in. The Westin Hotel in Calgary knows that business people are its major customers, and most business people have heard of the *One Minute Manager*. The hotel, therefore, calls its feedback form the 60 Second Critic, and, importantly, it really has been designed to take only 60 seconds to complete.

It is more unusual for restaurants to have fill-in feedback cards for customers, although it is increasingly common in the USA and Canada. Fourth Street Rose in Calgary has one we like because if you fill it in, the card goes in a monthly draw and the winner gets a free meal for four at the restaurant.

Kwik-Fit give cards to all customers to fill in and get 12,000 per month returned, approximately 5% of all business.

SAS get our accolade for the most fun feedback device we have yet seen. Each passenger is given a brochure which is divided into three lateral segments. These have to be manipulated like a Chinese puzzle to get you from page 1 through to page 4.

It's fascinating watching passengers working out how to get into their brochures. Complete strangers begin to talk and help one another to crack the entry puzzle.

Once the passengers have got to page 4 there are 3 coloured discs each of which can be pulled off. Passengers are asked to rate the quality of the cabin crew service on their flight and before disembarking to stick one of the discs on the seat back facing them. Each colour represents a different rating – excellent, average, poor. The crew then pick off all the discs at the end of the flight and assess their performance during that trip.

Responding to complaints is another moment of truth

What do you do when you receive a written or verbal complaint?

We reproduce an example from Lifeskills' professional complainer, John Dodds! But, joking aside, all businesses should pray to have customers like John, because he is one of the 4% who do complain.

John's developing relationship with the Heathrow Penta Hotel

14 December 1987

Dear Mr Dodds

Thank you for completing a Guest Questionnaire after your stay with us this month. I am very glad to hear that, in general, you were satisfied with our services.

I was concerned to note your comments regarding the lack of heat and hot water in Room 3047. I have asked our Chief Engineer to carry out a full investigation, in order that remedial action can be taken. We do normally supply spare blankets in our bedrooms and I have asked the Executive Housekeeper to ensure that there is one in future.

I do apologise for the poor service you experienced in the Coffee Shop and I have brought this to the attention of the Department Head concerned.

Please accept my sincere apologies for these inadequacies and I do hope that you will stay with us again and give us an opportunity to show that we can do better.

Constructive comments are always extremely useful and I am most grateful for the trouble you have taken.

Yours sincerely
General Manager

6 January 1988

Dear Mr Dodds

Thank you once again for filling in a Guest Questionnaire. I am glad to note that your room was warm this time.

I have noted your comments regarding the service and can appreciate how frustrating this must have been. I have now spoken to the Food and Beverage Manager who will ensure that the waitresses serve guests individually and not 'school dining room style' as I understand from your remark.

Please accept my apologies for these inadequacies and I do hope that you will stay with us again and give us an opportunity to show that we can do better.

Constructive comments are always extremely useful and I am most grateful for the trouble you have taken.

Yours sincerely
General Manager

15 January 1988

Dear Mr Dodds

Thank you for completing a Guest Questionnaire after your stay with us this month. I am very glad to hear that, in general, you were satisfied with our services.

We are presently negotiating a completely new in-house entertainment system which we hope to install within the next two or three months.

Constructive comments are always extremely useful and I look forward to welcoming you back again to the hotel.

Yours sincerely
General Manager

How to handle complaints when you get them

'A customer with the passion to get angry also has the ability to be loyal.'

Michael LeBoeuf

We can work hard to ensure that, as providers of service, we approach our customers from quadrant 4. As we have realised however, there are no guarantees that that is where our customers will come from! If they are quadrant 4 people you have a flying start; if they are not, there is work ahead!

Not everything will go consistently as we plan it. In service, also, not every customer comes with the same expectations. Given those realities, however hard you work, you will not please all the people all the time! At some time people will wish to complain about your service. This is normal and you should expect it.

At that moment again, attitude is the key to success. It is not easy to listen to criticism, particularly if it is not made skilfully. It is easy to be dismissive or defensive and to ignore or retaliate. If we are observant enough we will be able to detect our 'self-talk'. We all talk to ourselves in our heads, and tell ourselves things which may produce problems. Self-talk can be positive or negative. We will respond and react as a result of what we tell ourselves. The appropriate self-talk when managing complaints could be:

- 'I wish that had not happened, but I am pleased the client has told me as this gives me a second chance.'

- 'A complaint is a moment of truth, a service opportunity.'

> *Nobody ever wins an argument with a customer.*

- 'This is not pleasant to hear, but it is a chance to learn!'

On hearing a complaint we can respond in one of three ways. Our response may be:

Aggressive (Quadrant 1)

We express our opinions and feelings so forcibly that the customer feels threatened, punished or put down. Our intention, when we are behaving like this, is to get our own way no matter what the consequences. To achieve this we can be verbally violent, manipulative or devious. If we win and get what we want the customer may be left with feelings of bitterness, resentment or frustration. Because we have caused the customer to lose, s/he may want revenge and tell people about the experience.

Passive (Quadrant 3)

Here we avoid the issue, running away or ducking problems rather than facing them and solving them. This is servility. We allow ourselves to be treated without dignity or rights. The likely outcome of this is that we will emerge feeling bad about ourselves and the customer whom we will blame for our discomfort.

Assertive (Quadrant 4)

Being assertive means that we are confident, we face the issue, we recognise the customer's right to complain, and welcome the fact that s/he has done so. We accept responsibility without crawling and seek a Win/Win solution that will satisfy the customer and please us because it is also in our interests.

Service teams or companies that are successfully assertive become well-known for the effective management of complaints. They savour complaints and don't shun them!

Experience suggests that the following should be included in any set of guidelines on managing complaints:

- recognise the customer's feelings and listen carefully;

- collect all the data and details;

- accept responsibility; don't pass the buck;

- find out what the customer wants, work out what you can do and do it *quickly*;

- if there are things you can't do, say so and explain why;

- work out how to give that little bit more;

- don't, whatever the provocation, argue with your customer;

> At a top London hotel I ordered drinks for two friends and a mineral water for myself. The waiter returned with two drinks only. I asked for my mineral water. He told me I never ordered one and looked very cross. I insisted that I had. He again denied it. I insisted, and being in the service business was getting intrigued at what the outcome to this ping-pong match might be. Finally, he said, 'You want a mineral water,' I said, 'Yes please, just as I ordered.' He turned his back on me and as he stomped away muttered loudly, 'He didn't order it!' He got the last word, but also the last order from me. I will not return to the bar of that hotel.

- check that the customer is satisfied and thank him or her for bringing the problem to your attention;

- work out what you (or your team) can learn from the experience and how you can stop it happening again;

- make contact, if appropriate, with the customer at a later date; maybe a telephone call or a letter to ask about their current experience of your service or product.

Setting up a complaints system

We have been looking at the skills involved in dealing face-to-face with customers. This is crucial, but just as important is ensuring that a proper system is set up to collect, monitor and communicate complaints.

The best systems we have seen involve:

- a method for logging any complaint at the customer interface; we strongly recommend a single-sheet complaint form. We reproduce our own as an example at the end of this Step.

- all logged complaints to be sent to a central source;

- the central source to record and classify all complaints, look for

---

COMPLAINT REGISTERED

Lifeskills

Call/Letter received by: Date:

Customer name: Copies to:

Address:

Telephone:

Nature of complaint:

Action promised:

When will action happen?

Person responsible to follow through:

Customer's reaction to promised solution:

How can we make sure this doesn't happen again? Any suggestions?

---

themes, analyse by department, time of year or any other variable that might be pertinent to the organisation;

- the complaints analysis would be fed back to departments who are then encouraged to evolve strategies to minimise the likelihood of these complaints occurring again; these strategies are fed back to the central source;

- senior management are fed reports periodically, which summarise the complaints and detail the strategies employed to remedy them.

Give front-liners the responsibility
It is vital, however, that the initial complaints are dealt with immediately, at the customer interface. This involves giving front-liners

'Rule No. 1 –
The customer is
always right!

'Rule No. 2 – If
you find the
customer is wrong
then return
immediately to
Rule No. 1.'
Stew Leonard

considerable discretion, without feeling that they always have to check out with their managers. For example:

- The assistant at a fish and chip shop in Leeds who can give you an extra piece of fish if you complain that your portion is too small.

- The consultant who can reduce the costs of materials for a training programme because some have arrived damaged.

- The washing machine repair man who does not charge for part of the repair he has carried out because he believes that the part should not have broken even though the guarantee has just run out.

- The receptionist at a squash club who can offer a free game to an irate member who has been double booked.

SERVICE POINTERS

Stephanie was pleased with her new car from Lex Brooklands in Leeds and the way she had been treated at the garage. All questions answered, all purchase details made clear, the warranty promises specified. The car was immaculately clean and finished and ran beautifully with no sign of a problem. After six months she received notification from the garage to remind her it was time for a service. The card also said:

'We are pleased to inform you that the quality of components in our cars is now so high that we are able to remove certain checks from our service list.

'In future, therefore, we can promise you even greater reliability and from this service date the costs of all future services will be reduced by 12%.'

- **When you make improvements to your product do you let your customers know?**

One frequent flyer keen to build up all his bonus points in a particular promotion scheme understood that even though he had to change airlines on one long haul flight he could accrue his points if he kept the other airline's boarding card. He checked this arrangement with a ticket-desk attendant of the airline promoting the scheme. 'I wish I knew, sir. They have all these bright ideas in our marketing department but they never bother to tell us about them!'

- **How much 'internal marketing' goes on in your business? Is as much effort put into informing staff as it is to informing customers?**

STEP 8

STAY CLOSE TO YOUR CUSTOMER

Do we make it easy for our customers to do business with us?

Peters and Waterman in their classic book, *In Search of Excellence*, demonstrated that one of the major factors distinguishing the successful from the less successful companies was that of staying close to the customer. Remember once again Jan Carlzon's statement:

'If you're not serving the customer you'd better be serving someone who is.'

This means that within the organisation managers should stay close to their 'customers' – their staff – by walking about, talking to people, not solely sitting behind their desks and presiding at meetings. Similarly, staff will then be more motivated to stay close to their external customers.

How do you stay close to your customer?

All of the complaint soliciting techniques that we addressed in Step 7 are in themselves ways of staying close to your customers.

Below we list some additional techniques from large and small companies.

Dialogue with your customer – inform your staff (Jaguar Cars)

In 1980 Sir John Egan took over as chairman to discover that the company was losing nearly £1 million a week. He decided that the future was very dependent on the US market. He brought over 8 parties of dealers and amazed them by disclosing that he had identified 250 areas for improvement. He then hired a US market research company to carry out telephone conversations with several hundred customers each month. They talked to drivers who had owned Jaguars for 35 days, 8 months and for 18 months. Some interviews were taped. Many of the comments were unprintable, so the senior vice-president for Jaguar Cars, Michael Dale, sent the tapes to his managers. They passed them on to district service managers who then went to talk to their customers to see if their complaints had been dealt with. In this way the quality service message was hammered home to staff. By 1986 Jaguar's sales in the USA had risen from 3,000 a year in 1980 to 25,000.

Getting senior people into the front-line (Avis)

All managers, including the managing director, spend one week a year on the reception desks and washing the cars. This enables them to stay close to staff as well as customers.

Keeping your customers periodically informed (Stanleys)

This small dress shop in Leeds uses the following technique: when you have bought items from them on two or three occasions, the two sales ladies get to recognise you and begin to get a picture of your tastes. They then ask you if you would like them to telephone you when they get in something new that they think might appeal to you. Most customers are delighted to get this kind of individual attention. The sales staff really do ring up only with news about items that they think will appeal to that customer. They then give a full description over the telephone. The technique would not work, of course, if they persistently bothered customers with calls about clothes that were inappropriate.

Newsletters and magazines (British Airways, London Life, Lifeskills, Boccalino's)

British Airways and London Life are just two of the companies of varying size – 40,000 and 700 – who use newsletters and magazines to stay in touch with their customers. Customers like to receive these, so long as they are not solely advertising pitches. Although most of these

> *'Today, sales people are still selling products while customers want to buy relationships.'*
> Larry Wilson

publications request feedback and letters from customers, the communication is still largely one way, which is the built-in limitation.

You might argue, 'Well that's all right for big companies, but what about us?'

Lifeskills employs only 30 people and yet we send out two different free newsletters, one quarterly to 4,500 customers, and the other four to five times a year to over 5,000 customers.

Boccalino's is an excellent Italian restaurant in Edmonton, Alberta. It is brash, noisy, difficult to get into without a reservation. It is developing its image as an institution. So what does it do? It produces 10,000 free copies of its own newspaper called the Boccalino Times, full of competitions, news about staff, new promotions, jokes, endorsements, puzzles, photos of staff, famous customers, etc. Because people often have to queue to get a table, they now have something to read, talk about and have a chuckle. So if one restaurant can produce a free 4-page newspaper . . .

Treasure your relationships with your existing customers

Research has shown that the cost of keeping an existing customer is about five times less than the cost of developing a new one.

It is still the practice in some companies to pay more commission to sales people who bring in orders from new customers than if they get repeat orders or new orders from existing customers. The reasoning is that it is harder to develop new customers. That is correct, which is exactly why the sales people should be rewarded for spending more of their time with existing customers.

In a recent study in the USA, the Forum Corporation found that high-performing and moderate-performing sales people had roughly the same levels of product knowledge. What distinguished the high performers was their level of knowledge of the customer. That knowledge gave them the openings to use their product knowledge to best effect.

Theodore Levitt has been credited with the term *'relationship management'* as the new focus for marketing. General Motors in Canada in a study of its women customers, found that 80% said that, when buying a car, they were looking for a long-term customer relationship with a dealer they could trust. That was more important than price.

Larry Wilson, the founder and former head of Wilson Learning Corporation claimed recently that customers are looking for what he calls *partnering*.

'It's something like the way the best people have always sold, only much more of it. We're playing at a higher level, and we form a partnership with a number of people, and we make a long term commitment to it.

'When people have a partnership, they share values. They share long-term strategies. They share common visions. That's a long way from the old method of "17 ways to answer an objection", or "21 ways to close a sale". But most sales people today are not competent in creating that high level of partnership. They still think of their customers as opponents instead of members of the same team.'*

Creating partnership with your customer

● Visit them

Not just when you have a new product to sell, but just to see how things are going in their business. Senior line personnel can be required to spend a good proportion of their time (approximately 30%) visiting customers. Major customers should get at least one full day's attention per month, so that what they think, feel or need is never far from staff consciousness.

Support staff should have opportunities to accompany or work alongside customer contact staff and then bring back their experience to task groups, service teams (more about them in Step 12) or quality circles.

● Write or telephone customers regularly

Not to advertise a new product, but perhaps to check how they are making out with a previous purchase.

● Appoint a customer manager

Ensure that every customer is assigned to one of your staff with the prime responsibility of making contact with that customer at regular intervals. The appropriate time span will be determined by the nature of the business. That account manager should have the responsibility of informing the rest of the business about major developments and personnel changes relating to that customer.

● Computerise account records

The worst crime in business, arguably, is to lose the name of a

* Interview with Larry Wilson, *Training*, February 1988.

Good service is giving a little more than they expect.	customer. But ideally a customer record should not simply consist of name and address but: – what has been bought – how often the customer has bought from you – when you last contacted the customer – information on whether certain products are ordered and reordered at a particular time.

The survey of banks and building societies carried out by The Grass Roots Group* in 1988 showed that fewer than one in ten banks or building society offices asked for a name and address even in response to mortgage, home insurance, personal equity plans or travel money enquiries. Any follow-up, therefore, rested on the customer taking the initiative to re-contact the branch. This not only lessens the chance of a sale but it loses the opportunity of beginning a relationship which could eventually result in sales.

● **Offer a little bit more**

Make customers a special offer if they become regular customers; if they have bought an oven from you, send them a cookbook a few days later; don't send Christmas gifts unless you feel you have to – how much more of an impact to send a gift at another time of the year for no seasonal reason; send birthday cards, Christmas cards, congratulations cards, any cards; invite them to select previews of new products before an official launch.

Make it easy for your customer to do business with you, as they do at Christopher Pratt in Leeds.

This is a Yorkshire-based furniture and electrical retailer which has a policy of delivering any of its TV, video, or hi-fi systems and fully installing them. For technical incompetents like one of the present authors it is worth paying that little bit more rather than buying the same equipment from a discount store, spending hours reading the manuals, and still not getting it right. They also have engineers who do not set out to make you feel incompetent for having to use them in the first place.

● **Offer customer conferences and seminars**

Many companies hold marketing launches for new products, and this in itself is a good method for staying close to the customer. Everyone

---

* The Grass Roots Group's Major Research Study Into Customer Handling of Banks and Building Societies.

Excellent service is enjoying giving people a little more than they expect.

attending knows that they are being 'sold' something. We are not implying there is anything wrong with that, but at this point we would like to highlight an additional use of conferences and seminars.

Once a year the Hay Group, the international management consulting company, organise a 2-day conference. All their clients, world-wide are invited to it. There is no selling of Hay services, instead, top speakers from around the world are invited to address the 500 or so clients who attend on a pre-arranged theme relevant to business management. There is a separate spouses programme, the conferences are always held in impressive locations and the people who attend are usually at board or senior management level. The participants do pay for themselves. This is another example of customer education, and the benefits will be indirect rather than direct.

- **Offer value-added service**

Volvo has always emphasised customer service, and has a systematic programme of customer contact. When you buy a Volvo you receive a letter and a book welcoming you to the group of Volvo owners with details of all of the customer service programmes, such as Lifetime Care and the Careline service. Within one to three weeks you receive a letter asking if there are any problems, and your Careline card. During the year the local dealer might well make contact themselves with the customer, utilising Volvo's Selective Communication Programme which has details of every Volvo car and owner electronically logged and available through Volvo's own internal electronic mail system.

Next, there will be reminders to bring the car in for service, and there is a Volvo magazine twice a year.

After one year there is a further customer satisfaction questionnaire and this is repeated after the second year. After eighteen months you receive a letter describing the deal you can get by trading your car in for a new one.

The basic rationale is that after three years the only choice the customer needs to make is what model s/he will be buying. And Volvo's customer retention rate is one of the highest at around 70%. One customer's comment is that, 'You are looked after so well between purchases that it would seem like infidelity to buy from anywhere else.'

- **Customer liaison panels**

British Telecom are utilising this technique as a way of bringing BT managers and customers together. Panels are being set up in each of

Remember – the best way to sell products is to help the customer solve problems.

the districts in the UK. They are formed principally to discuss matters relating to the residential and small business user and to provide a forum whereby members of a local community could exchange ideas with BT management.

Each panel consists of around 12–15 members, including three BT staff and the remainder from the local community who have been identified as key local network individuals by an external market research agency. Members are appointed for two years which can be extended to five years on an annual basis. They receive only expenses for attending a meeting every two months for about two hours in an evening. Skilled group facilitators are hired to help the group run the meeting and reach consensus. Agenda items are drawn up by the independent facilitator in conjunction with the panel and with local and central BT management. These items have included payphones, complaint handling, performance indicators, marketing policies, phone books, etc.

All meetings are minuted and sent to Jan Walsh, Manager of Corporate Customer Relations. As a consequence, special Issues Panels are then set up to deal with a particular issue identified by one or more of the districts. These panels consist of the customer service managers from the districts who have identified the issue, customers from the Liaison Panels, a policy maker from head office, Jan Walsh, and anyone else who could contribute to the discussion. One example of an issue concerned what should go into the front of phone books.

To help the panels to stay in touch with one another and to get instant access to BT information, all members are supplied with Prestel equipment. There is a closed user group bulletin which contains all the minutes of all the meetings in all the districts. In addition there is a library through which members, electronically, can research into any issue that is to be discussed in a panel meeting. To begin with only 22% of members used the Prestel facility, but after one year, 52% now make regular use of it.

All the facilitators meet to discuss and swop ideas once every three months, and so do all the panel secretaries. A Prestel Forum also meets every three months consisting of a representative from each panel, two Prestel staff and members of BT's Prestel Implementation Group.

This is an excellent example of a relatively low cost high quality initiative for staying close to one's customers. There are financial payoffs too: one suggestion from a panel has saved BT £25,000.

Jan Walsh sees the process of the panels as being almost more important than the results, and she also highlights additional payoffs:

'The principles of co-operation and participation that the panels have developed extend into other management areas so that the company generally is focusing more on managing the customer's experience. You create an environment where customers and managers get together regularly to share the objectives and outcomes that both want. This all helps to move the total company towards being customer-driven.'

- ## User groups

Computer companies have been fast in introducing this concept, often encouraging specialist magazines for the Amstrad user, Apple user, IBM user, Apricot user, etc.

DECUS is the Digital Equipment Users Society, and was formed as long ago as 1961 as 'a forum for the exchange of information and ideas'. The membership manage the society and Digital provides a full-time secretariat, representatives to DECUS groups, and speakers and equipment for the various events. Users get access to DEC's international program library, with details of all public domain software and price reductions for Digital's own software. There are annual chapter conferences, training seminars and newsletters.

- ## Endorsements

Get endorsements from your customers when they are satisfied with your product. Ask them to write a testimonial letter on their business letterhead. If they are not sure how to do this, send them copies of other testimonial letters you have received. Compose a sample letter. Ask them if you can use them as references for future customers.

- ## Referrals

If your customers are very satisfied they will usually be happy to give you the names of other potential customers who might benefit from your products and services. The value of the partnership concept is that it should be two-way.

- ## Ethical conduct

Relationship management demands integrity. Ethics aside, some of the questionable tactics of earlier eras in making sales at any cost simply will not do. You will not get the repeat business. Having said that, we do not believe in putting ethics aside. There is evidence to suggest that business is becoming more concerned with ethics as a value and not simply as a pragmatic necessity.*

• Educate your customers

With many product lines, technology is so advanced that a major issue for business is to educate its customers to be able to get the full value from a product and not destroy it in the process. Customers need to be educated not only to use new products but to understand new practices. Sainsburys have produced a four page leaflet explaining the benefits to the customer and to Sainsburys of the new system of electronic scanning of bar codes.

Sainsburys, Asda, Tesco and now many of the other supermarket chains rate all wines on a sweet-to-dry scale so that customers know what they are buying. Wine drinking on a large scale is still a fairly recent pastime in the UK and buying wine can be daunting to the uninitiated. Many supermarkets now give a full description along with suggestions on what to serve with a particular wine.

Similarly, supermarkets are using the same labelling techniques to introduce new and exotic fruit and vegetables, including descriptions of how to cook and eat them.

Computer companies offer coaching as part of the sale, although sometimes the training is so time intensive it has to be charged for.

• Treat your customers as an appreciating asset

At our favourite Italian restaurant in Leeds we became interested in working out just what level of business each waiter and waitress handled.

Tom Peters in *Thriving on Chaos*** suggests a three-step formula for valuing the business handled daily by a front-line employee:

Step 1: estimate the ten year or lifelong value of a customer, based upon the size and frequency of a good customer's average transaction.

Step 2: multiply by two, to take into account that a good customer will bring at least one other long-term customer into the business.

Step 3: multiply the new total by the average number of customers served per day by the front-line person or group.

---

* Two books demonstrate this well: Ken Blanchard and Norman Vincent Peale, *Ethical Management* Morrow, 1988, John Elkington, *The Green Capitalists*, Victor Gollancz, 1987.
** Tom Peters, *Thriving On Chaos*, Macmillan, 1988.

> *You shouldn't aim to satisfy customers but to delight them.*

Using his formula for our Italian restaurant we calculated the average order per customer to be around £10. The customer visits on average once a month. Doubling this to take account of the referral factor gives a total of £240 per customer, per year.

We took a five year customer lifespan for the average customer, lower than Peters', which made the total per customer £1,200.

Each waiter or waitress serves around 80 people each day making a total of £96,000.

This means that each of those waiters and waitresses are managing £96,000 of the restaurant's future each day!

It also means that a waiter who upsets a customer who never returns has lost an appreciable amount of business. This formula may not apply equally to all sections of business but a major learning point remains.

Looked at like this the value of staying close to your customers, giving them a little bit more, managing all of those moments of truth through skilful application of the '4 Ps', becomes transparently obvious.

It also has implications for how front-line staff should be selected, trained, rewarded and treated. More of that in Step 11.

Methods for staying close to the customer – US style

There are obviously dangers in applying American data to Britain, especially since some US practices for staying close to the customer are not yet widely used here. However we did think it could be illuminating to present some findings of an American Management Association Report on Consumer Affairs entitled 'Close To The Customer'.*

Tactics (% of companies using)	*Effectiveness Rating (out of 5)*
Toll-free numbers (53)	4.08
Focus groups (55)	3.89
Mail/phone questionnaires (61)	3.75
Consumer relations training (61)	3.70
Consumer educational materials (62)	3.61
Point-of-purchase surveys (31)	3.59
Comment cards (38)	3.33
Assigning non-sales personnel to point-of-purchase (20)	3.33

The conclusions were drawn from 267 returns from a polling of AMA members and members of the Society for Consumer Affairs Professionals, and included data from 103 small firms, 84 mid-size firms and 80 large firms.

A reported 30% of toll-free number callers became brand-loyal customers. No wonder this technique scored so highly. There were drawbacks, however; for example some customers just wanted to chat generally!

Focus groups, involving structural interviewing of selected customers, were popular, but mainly with the large companies, because of their cost.

Interestingly, some of the most common practices in the UK, like comment cards and questionnaires, were rated lowest in effectiveness.

The survey also looked at how well a business's customer affairs departments communicated information on customer satisfaction and complaints throughout the organisation. They found that:

73% keep regular counts of customer comments/complaints

66% issue regular reports on customer comments/complaints

61% send reports direct to CEO level

65% track how long it takes to respond to a complaint

61% say that consumer affairs objectives are part of their organisation's strategic plans

only 34% include data on the competition in their reports

42% link consumer affairs objectives to the appraisal and reward systems.

It would be fascinating to see comparable British data.

SERVICE POINTERS

A couple on a journey in England visited a Little Chef fast-food outlet. It was very busy but they found a table eventually, and ordered their meal. 'Tea or coffee with the meal?' asked the waitress most pleasantly, despite being kept very busy by all the tables she was responsible for. 'I would like some really weak tea if that's possible,' said the woman. The meal and drinks arrived. As the customer poured her tea she noticed resignedly that it wasn't actually weak, having stood in the pot for a while before being brought to the table. She decided it wasn't worth making a fuss about. Shortly afterwards the busy waitress passed the table and noticed the tea. 'I'm sorry, madam, but your tea doesn't seem to be what you ordered. I will bring you a fresh pot straight from the kitchen myself so you can have it just the weakness you like.' The customer was pleased and impressed. About 2 months later she was on business in the USA and met an American executive who was shortly to take a holiday touring England by car. 'What advice can you give me on eating places close to the main highways?' the Englishwoman was asked. She remembered the waitress.

- **Can 'recovery' of a service situation sometimes be more impressive than getting it right in the first place?**

'After moving into my present house (a new one) I went through the ritual of trying to get the builders back to rectify defects which had become evident.

'I gave the builder a list outlining all of the faults (a "snagging" list) and he stated on several occasions that he would attend to it "within the next few days". Nothing happened for weeks. Eventually I went to see him in his site office and told him that I was dissatisfied. I also remarked that many of the items referred to the joinery which was generally poor in relation to the rest of the house, whose slates and stonework were of high standard.

'The builder said: "I think you're being unreasonable. If you had paid over £100,000 you might have a case but for £60,000 what do you expect?"'

- **Never put down a customer, for if you do, your customers will eventually put you down – where you belong – out of business.**

STEP 9

DESIGN AND IMPLEMENT THE SERVICE PROGRAMME

If your failure rate is one in a million, what do you tell that one customer?

IBM poster

Let us take stock at this point and see where we have reached in our steps towards success through service.

1 You have become clear about what specifically is your core business.

2 You know exactly who are your customers, what they expect of you, and how you can impress them by exceeding those expectations.

3 You have a clear business vision, which is very visible to the people in the organisation and shapes their work.

4 You can identify clearly the 'moments of truth' with your customers which decide their impressions of your business.

5 You are clear that quality service to your customers depends on quality service between individuals and groups within the organisation. There is a clear understanding of the service network that links all parts of the business and there is an appreciation of the importance of developing a 'service culture'.

6 You are clear that the challenge is to 'create your customers' experience' at every 'moment of truth' and make it impressive. It will be impressive when you achieve excellence in all the '4 Ps':

- superb PEOPLE SKILLS
- quality PRODUCTS
- attractive PRESENTATION
- customer-driven PROCESSES

7   You recognise the vital importance of soliciting and managing complaints, and you are committed to recovery and learning from them.

8   You know how to 'stay close to your customers', internally as well as externally, and you are prepared to let your learning from these sources shape your policies.

Total Approach

Having achieved this amount of clarity, it is time to gear up the whole organisation to become obsessed with quality and the customer. We believe that organisations who have blazed a trail in this corporate approach have a great deal to teach those who will follow. The key lesson is that to achieve significant and long-term commitment to quality service requires a total approach built on these principles:

Ownership

- that it is 'owned' by the **whole** company, it must not belong to any department or function, or be seen as an 'off-the-shelf' package brought in by external consultants;

- the role of externals is to bring experiences, concepts and strategies that are shaped, influenced and 'branded' by people in the organisation; it must look and feel part of your culture.

Business-Linked

- it must link the training and development of people to the business vision and show them their part in realising it;

- it must link Quality Service to performance management or the appraisal system and to the bottom-line.

Leadership

- it must be led from the top; the top team are leaders, marketers and models of the quality service philosophy and must realise their significance and role.

Front-liners

- it must establish the importance of the front-liners who 'create the customer's impression' of the company in every contact; all others must see it as their role to make it easy for those front-liners to give the customer quality.

Line-Managers
* it must give a key role to line-managers; 85% of what happens in companies is down to management so they must be given the tools to establish the quality priority; managing in a service business requires particular skills, and many managers are given the responsibility for quality and service without the training to support them.

Total Quality
* it must involve **everybody**; the message should be that quality is not optional, it is part of everybody's 'job spec' and responsibility; it must not be left to voluntary groups who are enthused to pick up the initiative;

* it must link the business present with the business future, integrating current initiatives, building on present strengths, indicating the next challenges;

* it must promote the philosophy of continuous improvement; the journey to excellence is a journey, not a destination; the need therefore is for a sustained, structured programme that is managed and developed as a central part of the business;

* it must lead to the development of quality service standards for every part of the business; quality for the external customer must be built on quality service between individuals and groups within the organisation, and standards must be visible for every job.

Research
* it must use research to learn from the customer externally, and the staff internally, about perceptions of quality and areas for improvement, and research findings must inform policy-making and be seen to do so.

Quality Delivery
* it must be a programme which **models** quality, as well as providing strategies for implementation, there must be no gap between the medium and the message; people must feel they are receiving quality, as they are asked to create it for the customer.

All the '4 Ps'
- it must recognise **all** the factors which 'create the customer's experience'; continuous improvement must be pursued in all the '4Ps' so that progress is integrated and balanced; staff must feel that the improvements that they are working hard to make will be paralleled by improvements in other areas, that there is a coherent quality service programme.

Follow-through
- it must link quality service performance to:
  - measurement;
  - appraisal;
  - reward and recognition.

> 'What gets measured, and what gets rewarded, is what gets done! Make sure you are measuring and rewarding quality and service!'

Results
- it must deliver the outcomes identified as success criteria at the start of the programme;

- it must provide a sustained corporate priority, which is perhaps the biggest challenge of all.

Steering Group

In our view the whole corporate effort needs to be overseen and managed by a key group of people whom we will call the 'Steering Group', though it has different titles in different organisations. Its name is less important than its role.

This group must:
- ensure it is representative of the whole business, so that no department or function feels 'left out';

- have a clear remit from top management to implement the quality service programme;

- have a clear appreciation of its responsibilities.

The Steering Group's responsibilities are to:

- organise the internal marketing of the programme;

- establish and maintain ownership of it across the business;

- design the customisation of the programme to fit the corporate culture;

- plan the training events to ensure the quality service imperative is taken to everybody in the business;

- ensure that line-managers are given a leadership role and the training to support it;

- plan the logistics of the programme to ensure the continued effective running of the business during training events;

- plan the route by which eventually service standards will become part of appraisal and the reward system;

- plan the channels of communication up, down and across the organisation, so that co-ordination and cross-fertilisation can happen;

- plan the on-going methods for measuring achievements and communicating successes;

- establish on-going research programmes so that 'learning from the customer' becomes a way of life in the business, and staff attitudes and opinions are continually monitored;

- harvest service improvement ideas from every part of the business, acknowledge these, broadcast them and pass for action those that are feasible and desirable;

- ensure that service standards are set for every part of the business and performance against these is reviewed regularly;

- ensure that there is an effective mechanism for learning from complaints, internal as well as external, and that effective recovery strategies are practised;

- require that quality service is a key component of all corporate induction programmes.

Corporate Training

We have seen most success where the following training events have been present to launch and support the quality service drive.

Top Team Workshop
This is usually a one-day event with these objectives:

1 To establish the link between the vision for the business and the quality service performance.

2 To identify the starting point in terms of current business performance against the '4Ps', and priorities for future improvements.

3 To recognise what can be learnt currently from customer and staff research, and consider the implications of this.

4 To identify the critical success factors by which the top team will measure the programme's achievements.

5 To clarify any parameters they may wish to place on the programme in the light of business realities.

6 To develop clear strategies by which the top team members will model, market and lead the quality service programme.

Line-Manager Workshops
These are usually three-day events with these objectives:

1 To re-inforce the link between the business vision and the quality service programme.

2 To identify and develop the skills of managing in a service business.

3 To introduce the concept of Quality Service Teams and a structured programme for service enhancement in every part of the business.

4 To develop team-leadership and problem-solving skills as strategies for managing continuous improvement.

5 To clarify the role of the Steering Group and outline the structure for managing the long-term quality service improvement programme.

Staff Workshops
These are usually one or two day events with these objectives:

1 To re-inforce the link between enhanced service quality and the business vision.

2   To identify the features of quality service, and establish the significance of 'moments of truth', and the '4Ps'.

3   To enhance the attitudes and skills that create a positive experience for the customer at every contact.

4   To identify the internal service network, and establish that everybody has a customer and everybody is a customer.

5   To establish that everybody has a quality service role and responsibility, to ensure that everybody recognises that 'You are the difference!'

We have worked with many ambitious organisations who have shaped this kind of approach to their business and their culture, and we have learnt from many others who have opened their experience to us. They all form part of local, national and international networks of people and organisations who believe passionately in a commitment to quality and to the customer, and are prepared to swop experiences for the common good. Quality service professionals tend to practise what they preach!

We are often asked two very crucial questions:

• Do you have to involve everybody in an organisation?

• How long does it take to achieve success?

Being consultants, of course our initial response tends to be to answer questions with questions:

• Who can you afford to leave out of a commitment to quality service?

• What will you use as your success criteria?

But we do have some views that we go on to share!

The Work Force
We find it useful to think of how many people you need 'on-board' to effect change in a culture. Our experience suggests the following model has some relevance.
In any 100 people in an organisation you are likely to have:

- 20 who will be superb performers, people who are the 'salt of the earth', those you would trust with anything, who will never let you down.

- 20 who will not be so impressive; those you have to harry, cajole, challenge, supervise and still they rarely deliver the goods. People in this group sometimes seem to consume more energy than they generate.

- 60 who could go either way. They will be influenced by the culture. If you can make it stimulating, ambitious, rewarding and motivating you will win their hearts and minds and commitment. If the culture is not like that you will lose them. The battle is for that middle 60! If you can get enthusiasm and commitment from the majority of them, you are well on your way to success.

It is not unusual, when quality service initiatives are introduced, for there to be initial cynicism, particularly where there is a history of failure or inertia or frequent change. This raises a very real leadership challenge. In one organisation we know, the CEO tested senior management commitment at a very early stage. Where he met resistance, he cleared out a whole swathe of management to signal there was no option in terms of a commitment to service. You either got in or got out! Those were drastic measures to meet a serious situation, but the CEO turned round the performance of that business so profoundly that it now has an international reputation for its service achievements.

The Time It Takes
In terms of the time it takes to make such progress we believe it requires a commitment of years. When embarking on a programme, we find the following model of skill acquisition to be extremely useful.

It says that learning a skill takes us through these stages:

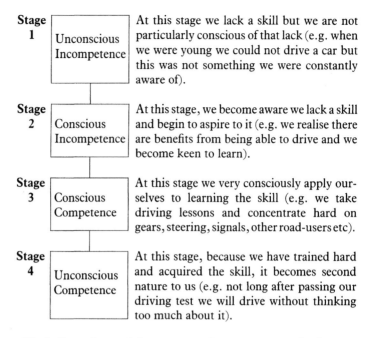

Stage 1 — Unconscious Incompetence: At this stage we lack a skill but we are not particularly conscious of that lack (e.g. when we were young we could not drive a car but this was not something we were constantly aware of).

Stage 2 — Conscious Incompetence: At this stage, we become aware we lack a skill and begin to aspire to it (e.g. we realise there are benefits from being able to drive and we become keen to learn).

Stage 3 — Conscious Competence: At this stage we very consciously apply ourselves to learning the skill (e.g. we take driving lessons and concentrate hard on gears, steering, signals, other road-users etc).

Stage 4 — Unconscious Competence: At this stage, because we have trained hard and acquired the skill, it becomes second nature to us (e.g. not long after passing our driving test we will drive without thinking too much about it).

We believe the model represents the process organisations go through in building a quality service culture. From not having quality service on the corporate agenda (Stage 1), through appreciation that it should be (Stage 2), through embarking on extensive training and other initiatives (Stage 3), the business embeds quality service in the fabric of its operation and the hearts, minds and hands of its people (Stage 4). Sophisticated service organisations of course say that the model is a cyclic one. No sooner have you reached unconscious competence in some areas than you realise you are at Stage 1 in others. It is a never-ending process!

At this point it will be clear that quality service programmes do require investment, of time, of money, of people. The experience of many of the companies we contact shows that it brings excellent returns.

**If you think education is expensive,
you should try ignorance!**

Learning from experience

We have seen significant achievements in a range of companies designing initiatives that fit their culture:

- Abbey National trained 40 line-managers to train 12,000 staff over a two-year period in a programme called 'You are the Difference'. This was a huge success in preparing the ground for the flotation of the country's biggest building society.

- Joshua Tetley and Son Ltd is a brewery which is a legend in the north of England for its fine beers. Tetley called its programme 'Quality Pays', which was the title of a book the brewery's founder wrote in 1822. Joshua was ahead of his time, and the present company is ambitious to maintain that tradition. Tetley has established some 80 'Quality Pays' teams to ensure internal service quality and standards within the brewery, to ensure its continued high reputation amongst northern leisure seekers.

- The Leeds Permanent Building Society has taken a series of steps to enhance its already high reputation for service. Pursuing a theme of 'empowering' those closest to the customer, it has established eight area Steering groups to co-ordinate the work of some 600 'Customer First' teams. These teams are addressing quality service improvements in their part of the business, while branches are being reconfigured to give more space and comfort to the customer. At the same time, having established how much home-buyers hate the pain and stress of acquiring a new property, the Leeds is offering its 'Home Arranger' service. Specially trained staff offer 'that little bit more', not just a mortgage, but help with dealing with estate agents, solicitors, surveyors, chains and all those other aspects of home acquisition that can be so daunting. Truly, an example of designing products and services 'from the customer's standpoint'.

- All service training workshops must be memorable in themselves. The programme must embody the concept of service in providing the participants (the customers!) with that little bit more than they expect. On the London Life programme, 'Working with People for Excellence', the trainers met the participants as they arrived for a two-day residential workshop and carried their suitcases to their rooms with them. In each room was a handwritten welcome card from the trainers.

- National Westminster erected custom designed marquees as temporary banking facilities at seven quality venues (usually country hotels or stately homes) around the UK.

- Ladbroke Hotels launched its 'We Care' flag on their forecourt. There was a ceremony for all staff, who had been written to at their homes, and a high quality, personally engraved name badge was given to everyone, along with a small gift (calendar or key ring) bearing the campaign's logo. All staff were then invited in a letter from the deputy managing director, to stay in the hotel and sample it as customers by bringing their spouses, eating together in the restaurant and staying overnight – free of charge.

• Gateway Hosts gave all participants a customised personal organiser at the end of a two-day workshop, with the programme's logo 'Who Cares Wins', containing all the service pointers that the course had dealt with. There was also a letter from the managing director and job information relevant to their business.

• And not only commercial organisations are engaging their people in the quest for quality service. Local Authorities such as Dudley and Solihull are training large numbers of people to enhance the quality of local services. The recognition here is that the whole purpose of local government is to serve the community which provides their finance and jobs.

An alternative approach to the large workshop format is to provide modular training in departmental groups or mixed smaller groups led by the managers who, ideally, will have been trained to run the sessions. Companies like Allied Dunbar, Unigate and Volvo have all used this approach. The sessions often revolve around a video specially designed for the company, illustrating typical scenarios which are used as triggers for discussion. They will sometimes involve customised planners or workbooks, and maybe even open learning materials for staff to work through on their own.

How can we release front-liners for training?
Many companies understandably are concerned with how they can train people and still offer a service. The Hong Kong and Shanghai Bank has trained a pool of 26 peripatetic front-liners who move in and take over while front-liners are being trained. They also act as role models for the remaining staff.

Setting up a system for communicating and celebrating service successes

British Airways produced a regular newsletter called 'Customer First'. This had stories of good service, photographs of service heroes and heroines, details of progress of service suggestions, messages from Sir Colin Marshall and other members of the top team.

Dansk Shell produced a video which recorded the achievements of the Danish service management programme. This was shown to all Danish employees and then an English language version was used to promote the success of the programme to all other Shell companies throughout the world. They also produced a magazine which kept people informed of all the service initiatives.

Setting up service 'jogger' systems

This refers to techniques to remind people of the service programme.

Poster Display
Putting up a new service poster each month throughout the workplace. People are reminded of the one-liners from the workshops.

Customised Personal Organisers
Traditionally these are the 'toys' of executives who have been on prestigious time-management workshops. Several of our clients used this format to house the workshop notes so that they would be kept visible around the workplace as reminders of the events and the key service concepts.

Abbey National incorporated a workbook into a planner for their two-day programme for all staff entitled 'You are the Difference'. This is like a time management system in that it has the diary, plus a section at the front which contains the company's vision, pages of tips on how to give good service, and pages specially designed to help particular job holders.

Everyone who attended a two-day service skills programme was given one. It came complete with course logo and customised pen.

Because it also contains a time management system it is, of course, in daily use and therefore, staff are reminded each day of the service programme.

Commemorative posters
Some companies produce posters of their own which are handed out to staff at the end of the service workshops. These are then put in offices, around the work areas, as constant reminders. The disadvantage of this is that after a while they become part of the furniture. A changing poster display gets over this.

We reproduce a good example of one, from Kwik-Fit:

I am your customer. Satisfy my wants – add personal attention and a friendly touch – and I will become a walking advertisement for your products and services. Ignore my wants, show carelessness, inattention and poor manners, and I will simply cease to exist – as far as you are concerned.

I am sophisticated. Much more so than I was a few years ago. My needs are more complex. I have grown accustomed to better things. I have money to spend. I am an egotist. I am sensitive; I am proud. My ego needs the nourishment of a friendly, personal greeting from you. It is important to me that you appreciate my business. After all, when I buy your products and services, my money is feeding you.

I am a perfectionist. I want the best I can get for the money I spend. When I criticise your products or service – and I will, to anyone who will listen, when I am dissatisfied – then take heed. The source of my discontent lies in something you or the products you sell have failed to do. Find that source and eliminate it or you will lose my business and that of my friends as well.

I am fickle. Other businesses continually beckon to me with offers of 'more' for my money. To keep my business, you must offer something better than they. I am your customer now, but you must prove to me again and again that I have made a wise choice in selecting you, your products and services above all others.

Designing a service suggestion scheme

Dansk Shell

They inaugurated a suggestion scheme as part of the service skills tutorials that were run. The response was fantastic – over 5,000 suggestions within a few months. They had to appoint a special task group just to evaluate the suggestions. Many were taken up, ranging from major decisions such as new uniforms for all forecourt personnel, to more simply designed invoice forms, name badges for all staff, personalised wallets for the tanker drivers to hold all the documentation – and which made them feel more important when they handed these over to their suppliers.

Toyota

One of the first large companies to systematically seek suggestions from its employees was Toyota in Japan. Japanese companies traditionally assume that the people doing the job are the best people to make improvements. In the UK we are just discovering this! To demonstrate just what we are up against and why we cannot expect overnight creativity from our employees let us present you with Toyota's record:

- 1960 Toyota received 5,001 suggestions (0.16 of one suggestion per employee) and 33% were implemented.

- Currently it is estimated Toyota receives 5,000 quality suggestions *per day* and implements well over 90% of them.

London Life
All 700 staff went through a two-day service skills course, a part of which was designed to send service suggestions back to the Top Team. Hundreds of these were produced.

British Airways
Suggestions were sent in to the BA newsletter *Customer First*, and awards were given for those judged to be particularly valuable. Many of the staff who went on the airline's two-day service skills course then opted to join *Customer First* groups. These were cross-functional and met about once a month. One of the functions of these groups was to generate suggestions. After the success of the service skills programme one of the suggestions which emerged was that the barriers of ignorance and tradition between the different functions needed to be broken down.

A one-day course called *A Day In The Life* was designed and all 40,000 employees attended at 100 people a time. A permanent conference centre was built for the programme including six portakabins. Each of the portakabins represented a different function, and participants passed through each of them in turn throughout the day. Each function had designed its own space and people who worked in that function were the guides.

People loved it, and understood far more about what everyone in the airline did and how all the functions interrelated. They also enlarged their group of personal contacts throughout the airline, and we do know that effective networking is the quickest way to maximise organisational effectiveness.

But doesn't something like this cost a fortune, you might well ask?

An exercise like the British Airways one is certainly not cheap – but look at the payoffs. British Airways is now highly profitable with a vastly enhanced reputation for service. Staff are proud of their company. Their aim is 'To Be The Best', which is the title of their new one-day refresher course in service skills. This is now run totally by

Market well inside and the outside will follow.

the managers, but of course is still a major investment of time and resources. However, there are no short-cuts to 'being the best'.

Canon
They began their Work Improvement Suggestion System in 1951 (although it was first known as the Creative Process Proposal System). By 1976 this system was producing 4,287 suggestions, or just under 1 per employee per year. By 1986, however, there were over one million, or more than 78 per employee per year. Oita Canon, the company's Kyushu subsidiary, recorded 195.51 work improvement suggestions per person in that year.

This, by the way, got them only fourth ranking in the nation for proposals! There are no limits on the number of proposals (other than that they should not be submitted by section chiefs and above) and in 1984 the highest number recorded by one individual in the parent company was 1,477 and the highest in an affiliated company was 2,125.

Finding a name for the programme

A service management programme needs its own identity – even its own logo.

We favour the notion of holding a staff competition to come up with the name. This helps to spread ownership of the programme.

National Westminster   'The Customer, NatWest and You'

Britannia Building Society   'Quality Matters'

British Airways   'Putting People First'

London Life   'Working With People For Excellence'

Unigate Dairies   'Who Cares Wins'

Glencoe Club   'Success Through Service'

Abbey National   'You Are the Difference'

Thistle Hotels   'Caring About People'

Computeraid Services (Datasolve) 'Service Excellence Through Training'

Lloyds Bank 'Customers First'

Joshua Tetley and Sons 'Quality Pays'

Volvo 'Do It Right'

The Leeds 'Customer First'

Letting the customers know

Some companies like to publicise what they are doing – British Airways, Barclays Bank, Body Shop, SAS, Dansk Shell, Glencoe Club, Avis, Jaguar. Others prefer to keep quiet about it, like . . .

Telling your customers you are training your people to offer ever increasing quality service can be very impressive, but only if you are able to deliver. Raising expectations and then not delivering will produce massive cynicism, amongst staff as well as customers!

STEP 10

SET SERVICE STANDARDS

Quality is remembered long after price is forgotten

The Chief Executive of one company we were about to work with on a quality service programme told us that he believed, 'Service is an art, not a science'. He wanted his people to be passionate about it and committed to it and did not want measurement or mechanics to 'get in the way', as he saw it. This is not an unusual stance and it actually represents a 'right-brain' view of service. Recent research into how we use our brains has highlighted the fact that each of us works predominantly in either the right or the left brain hemisphere. The characteristics of right- or left-brain thinkers are said to be:

Left brain	Right brain
Logical	Free flowing
Sequential	Whole picture
Data based	Feelings before facts
Looks at detail	Creative
Verbal	Spontaneous
Deductive	People centred
Rational	Pictures before words

Notice that one hemisphere is not superior to the other, they each bring up different gifts. The problem comes when we work out of one hemisphere, and close our minds to people who see things differently. Right-brain thinkers will be attracted by the creativity, energy and passion of quality service; left-brain thinkers will need the detail, the facts, the proof that it is working. Both are important.

We asked our Chief Executive:

• How will you recognise your programme is working?

- How will you prove to your Finance Director (likely to be an extremely competent left-brain thinker!) that your investment is worthwhile?

- Will you expect quality improvements in every part of the business or only where people are enthused and volunteer?

- How would you answer the question 'What do excellence or quality look like or consist of?'

Perhaps those were mischievous questions, but they do require a shift from right to left brain, and we do believe absolutely that quality service needs a whole-brain approach. We do have to move from passion and enthusiasm to detail, clarity and specifics! In all our organisations will be right- and left-brain thinkers, whom we need to persuade and motivate in their terms, they are our customers. This means we need to be able to talk standards.

If we visualise an advanced quality service organisation it surely has these features:

- a commitment to quality by everybody, at every level, in every area.

- an understanding by everybody of what represents quality service in the eyes of their customers (internal as well as external).

- a translation of those expectations into specific performance standards which are the basis of assessment and reward.

Service standards matter because they enable you to make concrete those factors which quality comprises. This clarity makes achievement more likely and measurement possible. Standards also provide a basis which can be upgraded at intervals, as you develop and improve service to meet ever-increasing customer discernment.

We believe these principles should, wherever possible, underpin the development of quality service standards:

- they should be decided after dialogue with your customer, and after studying the competition;

- they should be decided in dialogue with those who will work to them not simply handed down from on high;

- they should start with those areas of the business which most impact on the external customer, but should eventually address service between internal customers and suppliers.

- they should address 'soft' as well as 'hard' aspects of service.

Service standards must address both 'soft' and 'hard' areas of quality. Soft standards are the **people** side of quality. In British Airways they have learnt from their customers the importance of 'expressive' (soft) service as distinct from 'technical' (hard) service. In an airline hard standards refer to matters such as:

- time taken to check-in;

- punctuality of flights;

- time taken to get customers' baggage to them;

- numbers of staff on duty and available etc.

Soft standards address matters such as:

- the warmth of a greeting;

- courtesy and politeness of staff;

- the use of a passenger's name;

- solving problems for passengers.

These will have their equivalents in every business. Research evidence across a range of businesses confirms the importance of soft standards as a differentiator. It seems that hard standards, such as time taken to provide a service or deliver a product, have the capacity to dissatisfy a customer if we fail to meet expectations. They have less capacity to impress or excite if we get them right. Meeting expectations does not win us brownie points. Far more powerful for the customer are the soft standards that amount to quality attention, to being made to feel special, to being recognised and treated as an individual. Technical standards get us into the ball game; soft standards give us our best chance of winning it.

LEARNING FROM EXPERIENCE

An Airline

It was recognised that:

- Standards were vital because major competitors were working successfully to them;

- low staff morale meant likely resistance to anything from 'on high';

- decision: take evidence of customer research plus competition standards to selected groups who provided customer service in-flight and on-ground and ask **them** to write standards for their own performance;

- result: ownership of the standards document with a clear recognition that it must be the customer who writes our standards!

A Building Society

- Staff believed that customers wanted a reply within 3 days when applying for a home-loan.

- They put tremendous pressure on themselves and the business to deliver this as a standard.

- The Marketing Department carried out a piece of customer research which showed that only a small percentage of customers actually appreciated such a swift turnaround. A high proportion felt that they would have been happy with a seven to ten day standard because:

- this gave them time to re-evaluate their decison to buy;

- they felt it was more likely 'to have been done properly' with no short cuts.

The lesson: 'guessing' what will impress your customers can mean you are providing more than they want. Sometimes, of course, your customers do have unrealistic expectations and you may need to 'educate' them to appreciate the value in the service standards you offer them. Your thoroughness and guarantee of accuracy may be more attractive to your customers than speed of turnaround.

CREATING THE CRITERIA

We have stressed the importance of involving people in the setting of standards you need them to work to. This does not, of course, preclude the management input into standards which is essential. What we are advising is that standards are neither wholly decided by management, nor indeed wholly by staff. They need to emerge from the troika of customer, management and staff.

It may help to see just some of the standards that have been developed in organisations we know.

A Building Society (with thanks to Abbey National)

General standards
Managers and staff should work together to make sure the following general standards are maintained:

1   Be polite and friendly when dealing with people. Use their name when you talk to them. It creates a friendly, warm relationship. Express genuine appreciation for business or service received.

2   Give people your full attention. Do not talk unnecessarily to others when you are helping someone.

3   Take pride in your appearance. Dress with good business sense.

4   Keep the workplace clean and tidy and in good repair (in branches, pay particular attention to public areas).

Key standards of customer service
We all have a part to play in meeting these standards. They cover key areas of contact. If these standards are not maintained – perhaps when you are busy – the problems need to be tackled. Managers should therefore keep the situation under regular review and report monthly to their Line Manager on standards not maintained.

1   Interview/Meetings   Whenever possible and sensible, give your customer an immediate interview. If that is not possible, arrange a convenient appointment, preferably not more than 48 hours later. Be punctual for planned meetings.

2   Telephone Service   Answer the telephone within 10 seconds. Give your name and location. Record essential information. Avoid transferring calls. If you must, take care to transfer it to the right person. If you have to call back say when your return call will be made and keep your promise.

3   Correspondence   Aim to answer all correspondence on the day it's received. The maximum time for replying to correspondence is two days. Your letters should be in plain English, with accurate grammar and spelling. Typing and presentation must be excellent. Quote your telephone number/extension.

4   Enquiries (Branches)   Give customers arriving at an enquiry point your immediate attention, even if you can only tell them that another member of staff will help in a moment. Customers must not be left unattended at the enquiry point for more than two minutes without an explanation and apology for the delay.

5   Queuing Times (Branches)   Your customer should not be expected to queue for more than four minutes. Customers are discouraged by long queues. Please provide additional assistance wherever a queue represents more than three customers waiting for each open till. Arrangements should be made to open another position.

Your help in improving customer service

These standards may seem demanding. They are. Our aim is to provide the best service and being the best is bound to be tough. We will all gain by achieving these aims. They make a vital difference to our competitive position and the achievement of our business objectives. They warrant your full commitment and your co-operation. If you have any other ideas about how we can improve our service, please discuss them with your line manager.

A Sports Centre (with thanks to the Glencoe Club)

The bars and restaurants
We will:

- Immediately acknowledge (preferably by name when we know it) any member who enters the area;

- Offer a warm friendly greeting and show them to their place;

- Take their drink order, provide menus, inform about specials, and return promptly with drinks;

- Relate to each individual as s/he orders and thank them;

- Keep guests informed about length of wait and keep this as short as possible;

- If there is a problem keep people informed, ensure nobody feels forgotten;

- Remember who ordered what, and again serve with style and courtesy, use names as appropriate;

- Check out on quality/enjoyment after appropriate interval;

- Correct problems fast and compensate if necessary (work out cost-effective compensation).

We will ensure that:

- Customers are invited to visit all functions regularly. Their presence and their views are afforded royal treatment;

- Support staff are given opportunities to accompany or work alongside customer contact staff and then bring back their experience to service teams who study the implications;

- Customer studies and stories are given prominence in company journals or magazines;

- The customer's views are recognised as reality and are not attacked, denied or doubted. 'If the customer feels it, it must be right' is always the starting point;

- Customer contact is personalised, unless it is not possible to do that, and customer contact-time is proclaimed as the highest form of activity. Paperwork and bureaucracy must never be allowed to get in the way of that.

The sports shop

We will:

- Acknowledge customers by name and offer a warm friendly greeting;

- Check out needs and whether help is required;

- Ensure physical environment is bright, attractive and always tidy; no clutter, no storage in sales area;

- Have good knowledge of all sports activities and excellent product knowledge;

- Give time and quality attention to all customers; telephones and paperwork will not interfere with this;

- Ensure a positive closure to any customer contact whether a sale is made or not.

A final point

Standards need to be seen as the foundation on which you build. They must not be set in concrete and treated as immutable. Your business, your people, your customers are continuously acquiring greater awareness and sophistication. Your standards will grow as you do; ensure there is a process of regular reviews.

SERVICE POINTERS

A milk-roundsman had had his round for 12 years. When he decided to get married he inserted a card into every customer's letter box, inviting them to come to the ceremony and to the reception for a drink afterwards. The invitation asked them to join him and his new wife in a celebration because by their custom and loyalty to his business they had enabled the couple to get established and make the marriage possible.

'On my first visit to an up-market tailors I was immediately greeted and asked if I needed help. I explained that I was looking for casual jackets, size 36 and wanted to see what was available.

'I was shown to the appropriate department and the relevant sizes pointed out to me. I said "Thank you very much. I would just like to look for myself now – I'll shout out if I need help." But the assistant remained a short (and not respectful) distance away – just two or three paces. I felt his eyes in the back of my head. It was almost as if I were under suspicion of shoplifting although I am sure this was not his intended sentiment.

'I became acutely embarrassed and left the shop muttering "Thank you".'

- **Good service is not about being over-solicitous; it never goes 'over-the-top'.**

STEP 11

RECOGNISE AND REWARD SERVICE EXCELLENCE

'Excellent service is not about being 1000% better at one thing but 1% better at 1000 things.' Jan Carlzon

Service consciousness needs to be part of the decor, the fabric and furnishings of the service organisation. One key strategy for ensuring this is to acknowledge service achievements in the reward system. Since every job in the business is a service job, each job holder should be able to:

- identify his or her customer;

- state the service they provide;

- list the ways in which that service could be enhanced;

- declare the performance criteria by which service success can be judged.

Once clear criteria are agreed in key result areas they can become the focus for performance reviews and bonus schemes.

RECOGNISING SERVICE ACHIEVEMENTS

Pay increments are one way of recognising service achievements and these can be used alongside other strategies such as:

- weekly, monthly or annual awards for service achievement;

- publicity in company journals or magazines for examples of excellent service;

- carrying out a service audit, gathering a whole company picture of who has achieved what in terms of service performance;

- listing service achievements as part of company performance in annual reports and statements to shareholders;

- recognition and praise for a job well done, as an on-going management strategy.

Sheraton Saint Louis Hotel

When you check into this hotel in Missouri you are presented with a booklet of coupons. Printed on the cover is the following:

'As our customer, you are very important. Would you mind taking this praising coupon book? When you see any of our hotel staff doing something right or treating you well, would you get their name and present them with a praising coupon or turn it in to the front desk?'

Employees redeem coupons for points that can be exchanged for cash prizes, Sheraton T-shirts, coffee mugs, clock radios, sports tickets, etc. The idea has worked so well that staff have begun to give coupons to one another for excellent service received.

Get the balance right between financial reward and praise and recognition

It is not always necessary to offer financial awards for outstanding service contributions. In fact to do so is not really creating the service climate that is needed. You could end up with a totally mercenary workforce – 'pay me or I won't smile'.

On the other hand, constant praise without anything noticeable in the pay packet can also lead to a poor service climate: 'If I'm that good, why won't they pay me any more? Maybe I should think about another job if I am that good.'

Some recent research reported in that excellent newsletter 'The Service Edge'* shows that in Fortune 500 companies:

- 64% of rewards for service quality are monetary; 46% are other merchandise;

---

* Published monthly by Lakewood, 50 S. Ninth St. Minneapolis MN55402, USA.

- 75% currently are based on individual performance, but the future is very much with group awards as service is more and more recognised as a team effort;

- In terms of effectiveness it is reckoned that:

  – with cash awards you have to invest 12 cents to put $1 dollar on the bottom line.

  – with non-cash awards you can invest 4.8 cents to get a $1 dollar return.

'Catch people doing something right'

The phrase popularised by Ken Blanchard in the *One Minute Manager*, and reflected in the Sheraton Saint Louis Hotel, should be written on the bottom line of every manager's budget and target plan, because doing that, and rewarding it, will make the difference between average service and service excellence.

Ways to reward other than cash:

– a handwritten note
– a public verbal statement
– a public written statement, recognising achievement
– a certificate
– employee of the month award
– photographs on the wall
– award of a special pen, mug, T-shirt, etc.
– change in title
– bunch of flowers, chocolates
– invitation to lunch at your expense
– special card
– vouchers to visit beauticians, health clubs, etc.
– time off
– more flexible working hours
– gift certificate
– the hire of a luxury car for a week
– theatre or sports ticket
– weekend at a top hotel for the recipient and spouse
– trips abroad.

The better you know your staff the more you will know what will be the right reward for each of them.

> *'Until you can write down the standards of technical and personal performance which will please your customer then you may not achieve them. Individuals and departments need to know exactly what is expected of them.'*
> Karl Albrecht and Ron Zemke★

Once there is a clear focus on service, it can be related to the career development process. At the recruitment stage service attitudes and skills can be sought as essential qualifications and service performance can be one of the elements in promotion.

In their own appraisals managers can be assessed on how far they have raised service standards in their departments.

A strong service culture will build up its heroes, heroines and legends. Stories will be told and retold of those who made a difference, those who were larger than life, those who pushed back the frontiers of service, and management's task will be to build the plinths and focus the floodlights so that all may see the standards these heroes and heroines set.

Service providers will realise that the company is serious about quality service when the company is prepared to pay for it

Rank Xerox

Rank Xerox have introduced a scheme which is believed to be the first of its kind, by which customers' views determine the pay rises of top European executives.

Up to 500 customers in each European country are asked whether they are satisfied with Rank Xerox's products and services, whether they would buy more products from the company and whether they would recommend a Rank Xerox product to a business associate. Another survey measures customer loyalty, investigating how many customers each national subsidiary has retained over the past year.

The top 6 executives in the company's 15 European subsidiaries will then receive rises varying from 0 to 8%, depending on the results. A weighted average of the results applicable to the various subsidiaries will govern the rises paid to the 40 most senior executives in the company's European headquarters in England.

A further 135 senior managers are rewarded on customer loyalty and improved customer satisfaction measured against the competition. Customer satisfaction results affect the bonuses of all staff in some way. Every Rank Xerox customer is surveyed annually as well as 90 days after an installation and the feedback drives the company's most impressive commitment to quality.

★ *Service America*, Karl Albrecht and Ron Zemke, Dow Jones – Irwin, 1985.

Kwik-Fit

Tom Farmer, chairman of Kwik-Fit, relates pay directly to customer service in two ways. Firstly, he lays down very clear standards to his 3,000 employees, then communicates this Code of Practice to each customer and, secondly, relates performance to pay, but with the knowledge that profitability can only be related to customer satisfaction.

A depot manager's guaranteed pay is probably only average, but he can earn in addition some 5% of the depot profits, which can increase salary in some cases five times. Now this could be seen as an invitation to a focus on short-term profits and hang the long-term consequences. This is where the Code of Practice comes in. Managers are penalised if there are customer complaints. Indeed, a manager can be sacked immediately if a customer complains that s/he has been sold a service or part that is not really needed.

Kwik-Fit's success relies heavily on this real focus of customer satisfaction and financial reward. Their managers are not set budgets. They have a system called Target +, which states simply that their target is to do better than their previous best month. If, for example, a depot makes £100,000 in its best month for the previous few months, its target for the next month is to better that. If the depot makes £110,000, the 5% of the increase of £10,000 (i.e. £500) goes directly to the manager as a bonus. The target for the next month then becomes half of the previous increase, i.e. £105,000 . . . and so on.

In addition to this, Kwik-Fit have an award scheme called *Going For Gold*, which hammers home the standards that are expected. The programme starts on 1 November each year and consists of three-month periods. If a depot receives a complaint within month one, their period starts again on the first of the following month, and so on. Depots that receive zero complaints over three months or more get the following awards:

Bronze award
– 3 months complaint-free
If your Centre achieves 'zero complaints' over a period of 3 months you will receive the 'Bronze Award':

Bronze medal and plaque for display in the centre
Dinner for all centre staff

Silver award
– 6 months complaint-free
If your Centre achieves 'zero complaints' over a period of 6 months you will receive the 'Silver Award':

Silver medal and plaque for display in your centre
Dinner for all centre staff and their partners

Gold award
– 9 months complaint-free
If your Centre achieves 'zero complaints' over a period of 9 months you will receive the 'Gold Award':

Gold medal and plaque for display in your centre
Dinner for all team members and partners
Gold sovereign for each team member, currently worth approx. £50

The results of these schemes are published in a special newsletter called *Customer Care*, which includes the names of the depots which have received complaints. If a depot has, for example, a gold plaque and then receives a complaint, the plaque is immediately and ceremoniously taken down.

The complaints are ones that are identified through the customer service cards or the telephone monitoring service and they will always be 'controllable complaints', that is, any expression of dissatisfaction by a customer – through a letter, phone call or satisfaction card comment – which relates to:

A   A code of practice infringement

B   Unpleasant or unhelpful staff behaviour or attitude

C   Poor presentation of centre or staff

Examples of these are quoted from the Code of Practice:

A1 – Failure to fit protective covers
   – Leaving grease marks on steering wheel/gear stick etc.
   – Handling car roughly or carelessly on forecourt/on and off ramps etc.

A2 – Failure to examine vehicle with customer
   – Failure to give *honest* appraisal of work required
   – Failure to examine vehicle *properly* and *thoroughly* before any work is done

A3 – Failure to give binding quotation *before* work commences
   – Failure to charge quoted amount

A4 – Failure to carry out work in accordance with Company's laid-down procedures

A5 – Failure to inform customer immediately about any compli-
cations or delays
– Misleading customer about time required to complete job
– Misleading customer about availability of parts

A6 – Failure to examine all finished work with customer before
vehicle leaves premises
– Failure to reassure customer about possible early problems
with his exhaust system

A7 – Failure to make available to customer parts removed from
vehicle

B – Failure to attend to newly arrived customers
– Giving unhelpful/rude reply to customer enquiry either face to
face or on the telephone
– Ignoring customer
– Being patronising towards customer

C – Untidy forecourt/reception area/workshop area
– Dirty/badly equipped toilets
– Switched off video
– Untidy/dirty staff
– Staff smoking
– Radio blaring

The workforce are very enthusiastic about this scheme.

Volvo

Volvo Concessionaires UK have had a similar experience with their
award scheme, The Alex Price Award. There are not even any dinners
or gold sovereigns to be had with this, only trophies, but the dealers
clamour to win these awards. There are 13 zone winners, and then
each of these competes to be overall national winner. The criteria are
firmly embedded in customer service:

- Customer retention policy

- Customer hospitality facilities – coffee, loan cars, courtesy cars,
etc.

- Innovation – highlighted by a real benefit to the customer

- Teamwork – demonstrated by specific actions on a regular basis

- In-dealership training and staff development programmes

- Telephone response and handling

- Role of dealer principal in ensuring customer satisfaction

- Published company policy standards updated regularly and circulated to all members of staff

- Dealership image and appearance

- Dealership involvement within the local community.

Volvo also lay down very clear identifiable standards with their Dealer Achievement Bonus Scheme. This scheme is aimed at evaluating the performance and standards of individual dealers within their own territory of responsibility. A dealer can score a maximum of 100 points on eight criteria which is then linked to sales performance. Customer service is the theme that runs throughout those eight criteria.

Having set standards they need to be maintained. Volvo have five-year contracts with their dealers, but these will not be renewed if amongst other things a dealership consistently rates low on quality of service. At the last renewal 50+ dealers lost their franchises as a result of their failure to meet levels of performance or customer service standards.

What we have seen in this step is that it is crucial for operational standards of service excellence to be set. We have seen how these standards can be set directly from the top, as with Kwik-Fit and Volvo, or by involving staff themselves, as at the Glencoe Club in Calgary.

Linking Reward to Service Improvement

Some of the things you should bear in mind when designing a service incentive scheme:

- Keep it simple – we should not need a maths degree to work out how we benefit from achieving service excellence;

- Balance the benefits – make sure it's good for the business as well as the staff, it rewards teams as well as individuals;

- Make it immediate – relate it to day to day performance, waiting too long will take the edge off it.

- Let the customer do the rating whenever possible – next best would be peer rating, least best is management choice.

- Involve staff in the scheme design – it will be much better for that in so many ways.

- Link reward to standards that are MARS (Measurable, Achievable, Realistic, Specific.)

- Ensure it applies to everybody and reinforces the service culture.

- Use a range of measures and measure what people can influence.

- Ensure that everybody knows:
    - the value of one customer's loyalty.
    - the cost of one customer lost.

One company has the following printed on all its pay slips:

'Sent to you by your customer'

TRAINING: A REWARD AND AN INVESTMENT

We gave an example earlier about how a waiter in a Leeds Italian restaurant is responsible each day for around £96,000 of business. If our front-liners are so important, then why are they the most poorly paid, less well trained and treated with less dignity than most other staff, many of whom come nowhere near an actual customer?

Your receptionist is one of the key people in your company. How much time did you spend on selection?

How much training do you give any of your staff who answer the telephone to external and internal calls?

Have you ever considered training your car drivers, lift operators, security staff, doormen, counter clerks, housemaids, waiting staff, bar staff, shop assistants, delivery staff, etc. in service skills?

Try the three-step formula that we demonstrated in Step 8 for a restaurant waiter, and then ask yourself whether you want the future of your company in the hands of untrained people working for minimum wages.

The offer of training in itself can be rewarding. The message is: 'We think you are worth investing time and money on; you are important to our business.'

In the UK the training that we give our managers is pitiful. More than half of British companies make no provision at all for management training. Three quarters of companies of between 20 to 44 employees do no management training. In companies with less than 1,000 people, less than one manager in ten did any training.*

In the UK companies spend on average £200 per person, per year on training. In the USA it is £1500, in Germany it is £4,000. The USA, France and Germany spend between 2 and 3% of revenue on training. In Britain we spend 0.15%. A recent piece of research into how companies could retain their best people showed that the two most significant factors that make people want to stay are:

- the quality of communication in the organisation
- the availability of development opportunities.

People will stay where they are respected, kept in the picture, and have the chance to better themselves.

A survey conducted by Cooper & Lybrand found that high performing companies have 8.9 days training per employee a year while low performers trained their people for only 2.8 days per year. The high performers have increased their training by 25% in five years, while the low performers have cut their training by 20%.

Japanese companies invest enormously in training. Hitachi alone spends £30 million a year on its 165,000 employees, not including on-the-job training.

Almost certainly our front-liners are even more poorly treated than management. When we at Lifeskills run service skills programmes for companies it is not unusual to find that for many participants it is their first ever training course.

Service training needs to encompass everyone at all levels. It is a *total programme*.

Treat your staff as an appreciating asset

The know-how that your staff possess about your customers, products and practices is invaluable. The longer they are with you the greater the know-how – providing that staff are developed and rewarded appropriately.

Celebrate service success

Before people can celebrate a success they have to know about it.

---

* From Ian Mangham & M S Silver, *Management Training: Context and Practice*, University of Bath, 1986

SUCCESSLINE

How do you communicate your successes? You may not wish to fire off a cannon each time like Dana Corporation in the US, but you need to do something.

Even in a small company like Lifeskills we find that word of mouth is insufficient to communicate our successes. We also believe that all successes should be communicated, ranging from landing a new training contract to dealing skilfully with a customer's complaint, or re-designing the invoice form to make it more user-friendly, or negotiating a discount off the purchase of pens, or producing an excellent newsletter, or providing an idea for improving the quality of a product.

We have a sheet called Successline, which anyone can send to the rest of the staff, or if someone is bashful their manager will pen a Successline on behalf of the person or people concerned.

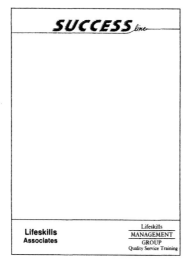

In Selfridges department store improvements in service quality are detected by customer and management observation and also through mystery shopper projects. Individual members of staff who have excelled in terms of service are awarded bottles of champagne at high profile ceremonies conducted by senior managers.

In larger companies there are in-house magazines and newsletters. These need to shout out about the service heroes and heroines.

All service suggestions should be acknowledged, and those that are implemented rewarded in some way – not necessarily financially.

Annual reports can make it clear to staff how the service programme has contributed to profits and image and customer satisfaction.

If you are unsure how to celebrate successes ask some of your staff. They will come up with creative ideas and organise them for you too!

SERVICE POINTERS

An old man, dignified but obviously down on his luck, joined the queue of Bryan's fish and chip shop in Leeds. When his time came he said quietly, 'I would like some fish and chips, but I have no money at the moment. I will give you this set of screwdrivers in exchange for some.' He produced some screwdrivers, used but once, of reasonable quality, and offered them to an uncertain counter assistant. The shop owner had overheard this transaction and came across quickly. He said quietly, 'That's all right sir, you are welcome to some fish and chips and we'd like you to keep those screwdrivers, they look good ones and you may need them in the future.' The old man persisted in this offer and some of the queue began to giggle with embarrassment at the incident. 'Please get this gentleman what he ordered,' the owner told his assistant. He came round to the front of the counter, gently took the man's arm, lifted the pack of fish and chips and said, 'Let's go outside sir. There's a seat outside the shop and you can eat these while they are hot'. They walked out together and the shop owner sat outside and talked over 'the old days' with the man as he ate his meal. He came back once to get some salt and vinegar which the old man welcomed. The sight of them sitting like old friends outside changed the queue's embarrassed giggles to appreciative conversations. The staff served other customers with even more enthusiasm for the rest of the evening and the story was told and re-told around the neighbourhood for weeks.

- **Can you think of other examples where a service story became a self-generating advertising exercise?**

'Buying an electric blanket for my mother I had selected the one I wanted and made my way to a till which was lit as a paystation.

'As I reached the till the cashier finished serving another customer, shut the drawer and walked away. There was no explanation but as the sign was still lit up I waited – and waited.

'Over a period of 3–4 minutes two other potential customers joined me, all of us with our goods in our hands – two members of staff passed us but said or did nothing.

'After a period of almost five minutes with no staff approaching and no other paydesk nearby I put the box containing the blanket on the desk and walked away. It was only £25 in cost, but I did not need that store's business.

'I looked back as I left the store and noticed that one of the other customers had done the same as me.

'I went straight into a nearby store and bought the same article (for £1 more) but was treated quickly and courteously.'

- **How well was this store managing the customer's experience? What could it do in terms of the '4 Ps' to improve the service?**

STEP 12

DEVELOP THE SERVICE PROGRAMME

A satisfied customer is a living, walking advertisement for your business

Those companies who re-committed to quality service during the 1980s have a great deal to teach those who will face the challenge in the 1990s.

Research carried out in 1989 by Management Centre Europe (MCE) indicated that service will be a major business priority for the 1990s. MCE surveyed over a thousand Senior Managers across fourteen European countries, 54% from manufacturing, 46% from service companies. The survey revealed that:

- 94% say service will be a major business issue over the next 5 years;

- 78% say it is **the** key to competitive success;

but at the same time:

- only 56% say they work in companies which have service as a corporate priority;

- only 38% are in companies who have done any management training on the theme of service;

- only 28% train non-management personnel;

- only 24% analyse the competition;

- 51% report on customer satisfaction;

- only 39% seek to eliminate bureaucracy that impairs service;

- 47% have customer service included in job descriptions and performance standards.

A similar survey reflected a parallel situation in the USA. Of 3,300 senior executives surveyed, 80% said that improving the quality of service is the key to competitive success. Only 50%, however, said that service is actually a company priority, less than 50% of companies report on customer satisfaction, hardly any eliminate bureaucracy, and few train non-managers or analyse the competition. Interestingly enough, a survey amongst Japanese management showed that, for all their economic success, they believe service will be much more important in the next 5 years than it has been previously. So service is clearly on the business agenda for the 1990s. What can we learn from recent experience that will help make the programmes for the 1990s even more effective?

Basic Principles

We believe experience shows that these are the principles which underpin an effective customer service programme. The programme must be:

Business-linked
Quality service must be recognised as a bottom-line issue. It must not be perceived as an optional extra, something a business addresses at the whim or fancy of one or two senior executives. Those who believe in it must show those who are more dubious that it will bring a bottom-line return. They must show the figures that result from customer loyalty, from getting things right first time, from recovery from complaints, from word-of-mouth advertising. They must show the results gained by the SASs, the BAs, the BTs, the Rank Xeroxes, by Avis, Federal Express, Abbey National and many others in terms of bottom-line. In such companies quality service programmes are seen as an investment not a cost.

Led from the top
Overwhelmingly, the evidence is that the commitment from the top team is decisive. The visible leadership service-modelling and empowering of others provided by those at the top releases energy, reinforces effort, and convinces the doubters that there is no alternative in building a winning business but to put the customer first.

Central to the vision
A vision that inspires, that focuses energy, that guides planning and decision-making, must be evident to everybody at all times.

Integrated into management
Line-managers must see service as part of their management task. They must have the tools and strategies to inspire and coach their people in the ways of continuous service improvement.

Motivating for front-liners
Front-liners must see that they are key players in creating the customer's experience. They must be trained to deliver excellence, and given recognition and reward for doing so.

Research-driven
There are many ways, systematically and continuously, of finding out what the customers think and want, and letting this information educate and inform the business. There are equally effective ways of learning from your own staff how service and quality can be improved and managing accordingly.

'Without information people cannot take responsibility; with information they cannot avoid taking it.'

Jan Carlzon

Owned by everybody
Quality service cannot be achieved by fear and coercion, people must want to deliver it. They will want to if they feel involved, if they are given responsibility, if they can see pay-offs for themselves and the company. The programme must be **their** programme, owned by them, appropriate to the culture, addressing them and their jobs, developed and implemented by people in the business. Outsiders can contribute by helping you to 'grow your own', but your people must feel it is theirs.

Linking past with future
The starting point must be to recognise what has been good about the corporate past and what is good in the present. Recognising achievements gives people confidence to address what may need improving.

No organisation is starting from scratch; any new initiative must be seen as yet another step in continuous improvement.

Translated into standards

Quality service is intangible until it can be expressed in soft and hard standards for all parts of the business. Defining standards makes them infinitely more achievable and measurable, and allows you to build on them as your sophistication increases.

Measured

Only when you are clear what are your Critical Success Factors, as defined in dialogue with your customers, can you know what your priorities must be. When you are clear what they are, you must measure your achievements against them. Until you have such data on an on-going basis, you may be working largely on hopes and wishes.

Linked to performance and reward

Critical Success Factors for the business translate into quality service performance standards for individual jobs. In turn, these become the topics for performance reviews, and lead to reward and recognition schemes which reinforce the pursuit of excellence.

Linking internal with external quality

Quality service for the external customer can only be achieved when quality service exists between every part of the organisation. Excellence for the external customer must be built on quality for the internal customer.

Linked with other corporate initiatives

Progress in the quality service programme must be integrated with other corporate developments: for example, any corporate restructuring, job-evaluation programmes, marketing initiatives, introduction of new technology, and so on. The aim is a seamless garment of quality service, so every initiative must draw its rationale from the quality service vision, and integrate with all other initiatives.

Whole-brained

The programme must address 'hearts and minds'. It must invite passion, enthusiasm and creativity for the right brain, and measurement and technical aspects of service for the left brain, providing a holistic approach.

Managed and followed through

A Steering Group, representative of the whole business, must oversee the programme and its development; assessing achievement, broadcasting success, communicating up, down and across, supporting initiative, planning ahead, co-ordinating, resourcing, and measuring achievements against the Critical Success Factors. It must identify the next quality service challenges.

Supported by training, selection and induction

There are no short cuts to service success. Like most other things, it is 2% inspiration and 98% dedication and determination. It does require training to develop the attitudes and skills that are central to the approach. It also requires you to acquire talented people and provide them with a quality induction to your service culture. Tom Peters gives some simple advice about the kind of talent you should look for. He says 'Hire **nice** people! You can train them in other things, but you can't train nice!' This makes a lot of service sense. In a service business, people skills are likely to matter more than technical skills, which are likely to be easier to teach.

Addressed to all the '4Ps'

Programmes that are not aimed at quality enhancement in **all** the '4Ps' will fall short of a total approach. Ask yourself whether your programme will achieve continuous improvement in your organisation's:

- people skills
- product quality
- presentation or packaging
- processes, practices and procedures,

and address any gaps. Our present approach encourages these stages in developing a programme:

1   Work with the top team to develop the Vision and identify their leadership strategies to support the programme. Establish the Critical Success Factors for the business.

2   Form the Steering Group and introduce it to its agenda for designing and managing the programme.

3   Collect external and internal research findings, analyse the learning, fill any information gaps, decide the implications for management, and the quality service programme.

4   Train managers as leaders of a service business; team leadership skills, problem-solving skills; offer a structured 12-step approach to service improvement in their part of the business.

5   Train staff: focusing on the key concepts, attitudes, and skills which comprise quality service; introduce the concept of service teams and the 12-step programme and establish that 'they are the difference' between the company being the best or one of the rest.

6   Establish Service Teams as a way of focusing line-managers and their work teams on service improvements. The focus for these teams is '1% improvement in 1,000 things, in your neck of the woods'.

7   Establish Special Action Teams to address service issues that are cross-functional or beyond the scope of the basic service teams.

8   Establish service standards for every part of the operation. Establish internal service contracts. Offer service guarantees which you can deliver to your customers, internally and externally.

9   Measure achievement against those standards, broadcast results.

10   Solicit and learn from complaints. Design recovery procedures, and establish preventative mechanisms.

11   Recognise and reward Success.

12   Ask your customers, and your people, 'What are our next quality service challenges?' Take these back to your Steering Group, your management and your service teams.

We have built this model and written this book on the basis of all we have learned from our customers, and from companies who were not our customers but were prepared to share their experience. They are continuously expanding the frontiers of quality service, but because they believe deeply in 'the cause', they are ready to give others access to what they are pioneering.

SAS

Jan Carlzon has built on the stunning start he made in the '80s. His leadership and the skill and dedication of SAS people turned round the airline's performance dramatically. The achievement was based on all-round attention to service detail. In our terms he focused on all the '4Ps'.

Product

He redefined the core business of SAS and its mission as being the best airline in Europe for business travellers. He eschewed buying new planes which were expensive and did not add to the quality of service for the customer. Indeed he has entered discussions with Boeing to produce what he calls the *3P Plane* – the Passenger Pleasing Plane. It will have more space to store carry-on luggage, wider twin aisles and doors for easier mobility within the plane and during disembarking, and reduced cabin noise. Perhaps most important, it will have no middle seats. As Carlzon put it, 'When was the last time anyone checking in for a flight requested a middle seat?' This is really designing from the customer's standpoint.

A major part of an airline customer's experience is the time spent at an airport. SAS and the Danish authorities are spending $800 million to make Copenhagen airport the world's most user-friendly airport. Once inside it will hardly be discernible as an airport, more like a luxury shopping mall.

People skills

All front-line people were put through a service skills programme. Carlzon himself believes that the content of these courses was secondary to the fact that staff could see that the company was investing time and resources in them. The new vision was promoted in a little red book, sent to everyone, entitled *Let's Get in There and Fight*.

He determined to 'flatten the pyramid' so that hierarchical tiers of responsibility were eliminated, and front-liners had much more responsibility thereby allowing them to respond directly to customers' needs.

The staff were invited to 'walk through walls', to break down traditional structures and methods that were adhered to just because they were there.

This involved much more manager training, because middle managers' jobs now involved coaching, informing, criticising, praising, educating, communicating. Their task was to translate the overall

This year's little bit more is next year's norm.

vision into practical guidelines that the front-liners could follow and then to mobilise the necessary resources for the front line to achieve its objectives.

Carlzon put as much emphasis on staff providing excellent service to one another as he did on providing excellent service to the customer. He himself spent half of his working hours talking and listening to SAS staff. When the airline had been turned around financially in one year, all 20,000 employees received a parcel in the mail. Inside was a beautiful gold wristwatch with a second hand in the shape of a tiny airplane. In addition, there was a memo outlining new, more liberal regulations governing free trips for employees, a second 'little red book' entitled *The Fight of the Century*, an invitation to a party, and a letter from Carlzon printed on quality parchment paper, thanking them for the great job they had done during the year in which SAS had vaulted from its worst loss ever to the biggest profit in its history.

Presentation

Even though the airline was in trouble one of his first tasks was to spend $4 million on new uniforms. Carlzon knew that if the staff felt proud to belong to SAS their confidence would pass on to the customer.

Processes

SAS are planning to provide daily connections all over the world, preferably non-stop or with a maximum of one transfer per route. They have established a number of centrally located hubs around the world in cities like New York, Rio de Janeiro, Bangkok and Tokyo. These central hubs will be linked with Scandanavia by at least one non-stop flight a day. At each hub, SAS will establish a form of co-operation with a local, high-quality airline that will carry passengers onward and non-stop to their final destinations.

They envisage a very close co-operation with the local airlines, who will have to share the SAS business philosophy. Timetables will be co-ordinated to ensure transfer passengers the shortest conceivable transfer time. They will share the same terminals for quick and easy transfers between planes and will provide similar service standards. In short, passengers should not notice the difference between flying SAS or with their partners.

As with British Airways, SAS knew that there is always a danger when you achieve success. The challenge is to maintain momentum, and offering the next Vision will be one strategy for achieving that. Now SAS have a new vision for staff to rally to:

1 in 5 by 95

In the age of the megacarrier, SAS know that they have to be one of the five megacarriers by 1995 if they are to survive and develop, hence their energetic exploration of mergers and relationships with other smaller airlines.

British Airways

BA have built on their 'Putting People First' programme and established their image as 'the world's favourite airline'. Their follow-up training programmes reinforced the vital role of managers in creating the new service culture. These programmes, 'Managing People First' and 'Leading the Service Business', were put in place to establish the management style needed in the new BA.

In addition, BA is dedicated to learning from its customers. Some 150,000 customer interviews are carried out each year to monitor service performance, and assess future needs. The results of these are made available to managers on a regular basis. This data drives management decisions and the choice of optional priorities.

As an airline, of course, BA are in the interesting position of not controlling two key factors which greatly affect what happens to their passengers: the airports they use and air traffic control systems they fly through. BA's development of Terminal 4 is a step towards being able to influence still further the factors which create their customer's experience.

At the level of service sophistication reached in organisations like BA and SAS you become aware that you have to make demands for ever-greater quality from your suppliers. You can achieve so much through working to improve your own services but where the quality of those who supply you impairs what you offer you have to get tough. When you buy-in the volume of products and service a major airline does, you are in a position to raise the quality performance of your suppliers.

What else can we learn from those who lead the way?

Build teamwork and a structure for managing quality

Advanced service companies recognise that quality requires teamwork consisting of teams with a range of purposes but all addressing service improvement.

Joshua Tetley and Sons established 'Quality Pays' teams as part of the line management structure in their brewery. Their purpose was to address service improvement for their customers, internal and external, and develop service standards for their part of the business. The Leeds Permanent Building Society is doing that with 600 branches. Head Office is devolving responsibility for quality service to Area Steering Groups and their branch network as part of its Customer First programme. Only essential support services will remain centralised in pursuit of 'empowering' the field to become ever more responsive to what customers want, when they want it.

In NatWest Bank there are over 2,500 'Quality Service Action Teams'. These consist of six to ten volunteers from each branch or department whose function is to keep the momentum of their programme going through the continuous improvement of service at local level. Over 300 training courses were held for the Quality Service Action Team leaders and for their facilitators. They meet for between 30 to 60 minutes once a week or two weeks, and if they have to meet outside work hours they get paid for it. The Bank was amazed at the numbers of volunteers who came forward.

After each team meeting a standard pro forma is completed by the team leader and a copy of this is sent to the Quality Service Department. On this is described the 'service problem' that the team is working on, and which stage of a 6-stage problem-solving model the group has reached. All this data is computerised so that, for example, the Quality Service Department could identify at the touch of a button how many teams in the UK were working on 'queuing' issues, who they were, and what stages they were at in the problem-solving process – extremely useful in monitoring the development of Service Standards. Regional Steering Committees meet monthly, and together with 14 Quality Service Managers from Head Office, ensure that nurturing and fostering of team ability continues to build on the tremendous enthusiasm exhibited to date. In 1989 the first annual conference for the Quality Service Action Teams was held.

The major emphasis is on local ownership of problems, as their market research showed clearly that over 60% of customer dissatisfaction was linked to local issues.

Quality is an essential part of their planning process, with every manager in 1989 having specific quality targets linked to their bonus and reward package. The importance of continually monitoring, and then exceeding, customer expectations and requirements is the underlying cornerstone of their strategy.

> *Don't be imprisoned by yesterday's success.*

Measure customer satisfaction and respond to your findings

BT now carry out some 10,000 face-to-face customer interviews and some 10,000 telephone interviews per month. They research customer satisfaction with some 40 service attributes which BT have established are critical to their customers. This research is so informative that BT are able to assess from a range of options what they can do in business terms to most impress their customers. BT's customers are informing and educating the business about what it will take to move and keep them in the Reasonable and Excited Zones of BT's Service Positioning Model.

BT Service Positioning Model

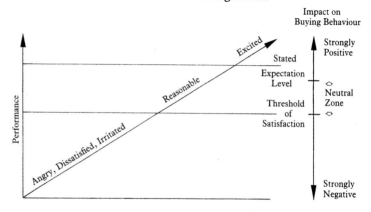

As part of its commitment to being a world leader in telecommunications, BT is restructuring its business to enable it to be even more responsive and offer even greater service to its 25 million UK customers. They will move from a structure based on geography to one based on customer focus. The pursuit is ever-increasing customer satisfaction.

Rank Xerox UK has similar corporate commitment. One of its corporate objectives is to 'be the No. 1 vendor in the industry in terms of customer satisfaction'. Through its passionate belief in quality, through its investment in training for 'Leadership Through Quality', through its use of cross-functional customer and quality-focused teams, Rank Xerox is advancing its market position in an extremely competitive industry. It does, of course, indicate its massive commitment to its customers by tying its reward system, especially for its most senior people, firmly to improvement in customer satisfaction. That really is showing that 'The customer is the boss'!

Aim for the top

All the companies we quote have impressed us with their approach to quality service. There is no blueprint, no easy route, just a great many clues as to what helps, and a need to 'do it your way'!

We have applied our learning about quality service outside our training and consultancy business. To show our belief in the model we describe, we have started our own home delivery pizza business. Some friends who are excellent restaurateurs have combined their food expertise with our knowledge of service. 'Salvos Pizza' is showing that the lessons of this book can be applied to businesses large and small. We are already seeing that you can achieve market differentiation through service quality even in home delivery pizzas. Our aim is to be the best in our business in our part of the world, and we can and do learn from 'the greats'.

Federal Express

Recently we had the privilege to visit Federal Express headquarters in Memphis and some of its stations. It is a most impressive operation and is outstanding in its:

Clarity of Goals

Three corporate goals: People, Service, Profit, are focused on with total clarity. Federal Express employs some 90,000 people worldwide and a very high proportion of them are part-time. Yet everybody can tell you the service standards achieved in the operation the previous night. Every station has a Service Quality score assessed against 11 Service Quality measures every night, as does the business overall. Fred Smith, CEO, broadcasts over a TV satellite network every morning to report to everybody in the company on the previous night's performance. Every part of the business has to know its profitability at all times. All bonuses are based on achievement against corporate goals.

Commitment to People

Federal Express says that nothing is achievable without its greatest asset, its people. It also shows it means it by:

- paying part-timers who work 15 hours a week for 17½ hours, if they are punctual and ever-present;

- giving part-timers 800 dollars a year to spend outside the company on their own education;

- giving full-timers 1,400 dollars for the same purpose;

- surveying staff every 6 months on how well they are managed, and attaching managers' bonuses to continuous improvement in the results of this survey;

- offering a Guaranteed Fair Treatment policy to all staff. If you feel you are treated unfairly, you take the case to your manager; if you still feel the results are unfair, you take it to the next level; if there is still no satisfactory result, you take your case to Fred Smith and another Director, who hear cases every Tuesday morning!

Commitment to Training
Every employee, every part-timer, in Fed Ex must engage in 4 hours training per month. Much of this is interactive video training, which you access in your own time. You are paid for time spent training and your manager discusses the results with you each month.

Commitment to Total Quality Service

- Three years ago, Federal Express 'played the percentages' in terms of the Service Levels (SQI Scores) they sought. They targeted continuous improvement, but were happy with results in the high 90%s. Then they asked 'How good is 99%?'

- Given Federal Express' volume of business, 1% SQI failure each year equals displeasing 25 million customers each year. They realised that at that rate in ten years, they could finish up disappointing the whole population of the USA. Their realisation was:

  - each customer takes a Federal Express failure personally – for that customer, 1% = 100%;

  - each disappointed customer will tell ten others (on average, re TARP research);

  - Federal Express' size and complexity exaggerates failure.

- They realised the only acceptable standard of service was 100%, no defects, no shortfalls.

- They call their programme 'Operation Zero', which establishes that perfect SQI scores are the only satisfactory performance levels.

- To achieve 'Zero', which many stations do, all service problems are tackled by service teams. These are of two types:

  - Quality Action Teams, which focus on eradicating service failure on their stations;

  - Root Cause Teams which look at strategic service issues, that are too big to be addressed by QATS.

These teams inform the 'Service Assurance Network', which is a management group overseeing the work of QATS and RCTs. In turn, this reports directly to the Quality Steering Group, a small group of very senior decision-makers who sign off on resourcing issues.

- Research over three years has shown that over 90% of Federal Express' customers are generally satisfied with the quality of service. The figures are used to challenge staff to even greater quality – the mission is 'Zero Failures'.

Communication and Recognition are key management strategies

- Fred Smith's daily 8.30 am worldwide broadcast on aspects of business is seen by everybody during the day;

- 'Bravo Zulu' awards (navy signal for a job well done) are given for examples of service excellence which exceed job descriptions. This award means the person's name appearing on citation plaques around the depot and a prize of one hundred dollars;

- For even higher levels of outstanding service there are 'Golden Falcon' awards (winner receives ten shares in Federal Express presented by CEO) and '5 Star Awards' (winner gets fifteen thousand dollars plus stock option).

- Great prominence is afforded all winners.

- Those who attain 100% SQI for one year join the '100% Club' and are given a four-day trip to Florida.

- Employees nominate from their peers the 'Image Maker of the Month'. The 'Image Maker of the Year' receives a citation and 2,500 dollars as an award.

- Customers are given 'doubloons' to award to Federal Express staff who provide service excellence. These can be 'cashed in' for work experience in other departments, a means of advancement in Federal Express.

- Federal Express trains all staff in its 'Customer Satisfaction Policy'. This provides a clear statement of what every Federal Express employee is empowered to do to satisfy an unhappy customer. Front-liners can provide refunds of up to 20 dollars, station managers can spend up to ten thousand dollars to recover from a service shortfall. The outcome must be:

'A satisfied customer at the end of every transaction'

- Federal Express have a management philosophy of 'Keep it simple'. One Vice-President commented, 'One SPC (Statistical Process Control) consultant almost brought us to a standstill, we should not have to be statisticians to be Managers!'. (This VP had been a part-time truck manager 14 years earlier.)

- Another Federal Express Senior Manager commented:

  'Our people hold in their hands our customers' perception of us . . . it's critical to our company's success that each person be as knowledgeable, as effective, as customer-minded as humanly possible. Customer-contact positions are the most important jobs at Federal Express. Employees in these positions must be the most posititive, motivated and the best trained people in the corporation.'

- A Federal Express courier commented:

  'At Federal Express, we are trained like astronauts!'

And, of course, with commitment like that you succeed: Federal Express won the USA National Quality Award, the Baldridge Award, in 1990.

The Baldridge Award
This is the US Government's way of attracting American industry and commerce to a commitment to quality and service. The feeling is that this is a matter of huge significance, as the US economy suffers from the competition from Japan and West Germany. Those companies who enter for the award report that it is extremely valuable just gearing yourself up for the application. Baldridge requires an organisation to prove quality performance in eight areas:

> *A successful company celebrates its success.*
> *But never sits on it.*

Leadership Testing management's ability to set quality goals, to engage in quality planning, to model quality and to instil service values. High scores in this area come from quality policies, carried through into implementation and quality management.

Information and Analysis This area tests the existence and use of data that measures and guides quality performance.

Strategic Quality Planning You score in this area when your quality planning is integrated with your overall business plan, when you use competitive and benchmark data, when you make quality demands on suppliers.

Human Resource Utilisation Your human resource planning supports your quality and business plans and is integrated with them. You engage your people in quality techniques, strategies and teamwork.

Quality Assurance of Products and Services You learn from your customers and let this learning drive the quality of your products, processes and service standards. You have strategies for continuous improvement.

Quality Results You score highly in this area by showing that you measure quality performance in a whole range of ways, by showing that you have corrective procedures for any quality or service shortfall.

Customer Satisfaction This is the major area of qualification for a Baldridge Award, comprising about a third of the total possible score of 1000 points. In this area you have to show that you know who your customers are: you determine their expectations and opinions; you select and train high-quality customer contact staff; you regularly measure performance and give customers service guarantees; you learn and recover from complaints.

Business Performance You show here that all your commitment to quality results in impressive bottom-line performance.

So Baldridge is having a huge impact on the quality service performance of many US companies. It is not respectable not to apply for the award, but to apply you have to attend to so many areas of excellence. Application is a signal you are ready to engage in all the dimensions of being a quality business. We congratulate Federal Express and all other Baldridge winners!

By the way, predictions are that by 1992 there will be a European Award for Quality and Service to equate with Baldridge. Will you be ready to apply? We hope these 12 Steps will help you prepare! May we wish you a Quality Future!

POSTSCRIPT – TOWARDS A SERVICE SOCIETY

All our work at Lifeskills is based on values and operating principles that we have lived and worked by since we began.

Our current vision in a single line is:

**Making a difference with
style and integrity**

We really do believe that implementing service management programmes will empower individuals and make organisations more humane, motivating, creative and exciting places to be.

If we recall that giving good service involves:

- Treating other people with dignity and respect;

- Being sensitive to the needs of others;

- Being honest;

- A commitment to learn and to develop;

- Accepting and rejoicing in the knowledge that each of us is unique;

- Believing that people respond best to quality treatment;

- Looking for the positives in people;

- Encouraging people to create their own visions and to grow and develop;

then those working for quality service are well on the way to bringing about a more caring, committed and communicative society.

And it all starts with such small beginnings – such as how we address our families, customers, colleagues and strangers each day. How well have you done today?

Whatever the answer, tomorrow can be even better!

BARRIE HOPSON   MIKE SCALLY
Leeds, January 1991

Lifeskills
International

Corporate Change Consultancy

Lifeskills is a training, learning and consultancy business with a leading reputation for designing, developing and delivering Corporate Change Programmes and Leadership Workshops.

Lifeskills can help you:

*   Gain Commitment from the Top

*   Establish the Company Vision

*   Undertake Customer Research

*   Train Your People or Train your Trainers

*   Ensure there is continuous 'follow-through'

If you are interested in Lifeskills' approach please contact:

Peter Gannon, Principal, Lifeskills International Ltd, Wharfebank House, Ilkley Road, Otley, Yorkshire LS21 3JP or telephone 01943-851144.

www.lifeskills.co.uk